WHY BOTSWANA PROSPERED

Why Botswana Prospered

J. CLARK LEITH

McGill-Queen's University Press
Montreal & Kingston · London · Ithaca

© McGill-Queen's University Press 2005
ISBN 0-7735-2820-2 (cloth)
ISBN 0-7735-2821-0 (paper)

Legal deposit second quarter 2005
Bibliothèque nationale du Québec

Printed in Canada on acid-free paper that is 100% ancient forest free
(100% post-consumer recycled), processed chlorine free.

This book has been published with the help of grants from the Canadian
Federation for the Humanities and Social Sciences through the Aid to
Scholarly Publications Programme, using funds provided by the Social
Sciences and Humanities Research Council of Canada, and the J.B.
Smallman Publication Fund, Faculty of Social Science, the University
of Western Ontario.

McGill-Queen's University Press acknowledges the support of the Canada
Council for the Arts for our publishing program. We also acknowledge
the financial support of the Government of Canada through the Book
Publishing Industry Development Program (BPIDP) for our publishing
activities.

Library and Archives Canada Cataloguing in Publication
Leith, J. Clark (James Clark), 1937–
    Why Botswana prospered / J. Clark Leith

    Includes bibliographical references and index.
    ISBN 0-7735-2820-2 (bnd)
    ISBN 0-7735-2821-0 (pbk)
    1. Botswana – Economic conditions – 1966. 2. Botswana – Economic
policy. 3. Botswana – Politics and government – 1966. I. Title.

HC930.L45 2005   330.96883'03   C2004-905808-8

Typeset in Sabon 10.5/13
by Caractéra inc., Quebec City

Contents

Preface

My association with Botswana began in 1985, on a short-term assignment in the Ministry of Finance and Development Planning. The next year I returned for a two year assignment (1986–88), which continued with repeated visits of one or two months a year to the Ministry of Finance and Development Planning, and then nearly four years at the Bank of Botswana (1993–97), followed by a return to the ministry in 2003. This study draws heavily on my experience as a participant in the policy process over an extended period and could not have been done without the knowledge gained through that experience. Yet I conducted the work as a faculty member in the Department of Economics, University of Western Ontario, Canada. I hope that I have been fair both to the Botswana officials with whom I worked and to my task as an academic, which was to seek out a full understanding of the forces at work.

The work has benefited from the stimulating environment provided by colleagues at Western who are interested in questions of political economy. A six-month sabbatical leave granted by the University of Western Ontario, spent at the Centre for Study of African Economies, University of Oxford, and supported by a grant from the Canadian Social Sciences and Humanities Research Council provided me with the opportunity to pull the whole together, while drawing on some of the documentary collection housed in

Oxford's libraries. The patience of colleagues in both the Botswana Ministry of Finance and Development Planning and the Bank of Botswana, as well as many Batswana in all walks of life, who educated me about Botswana and its traditions is especially appreciated.

I am grateful to Jay Salkin, who provided very helpful comments on several earlier versions, and to Christopher Adam, Jim Freedman, Charles Harvey, Derek Hudson, Keith Jefferis, James Robinson, Gloria Somolekae, Ronald Wintrobe, and Matthew Wright for discussions of issues and comments at various stages of writing. I am also grateful to two anonymous reviewers for McGill-Queen's University Press for their probing challenges at various points in the development of the argument. Seminar participants at the University of Botswana Economics Department, the Political Studies Department, the Botswana Institute for Development Policy Analysis, Oxford's Centre for Study of African Economies, the Institute for Development Studies at Sussex, the Canadian Economics Association 2000 Annual Meetings, and the University of Western Ontario have also been helpful. However, I alone bear responsibility for both the content and views expressed in this study.

Above all, I am grateful to my wife, who willingly repeatedly uprooted herself from friends and family in Canada to pursue my interest in development, and who, in her own right, shared her talents in many different aspects of Botswana life. Our children, initially reluctant spectators and participants in our Botswana venture, all came to share our enthusiasm. To all four – Carole Ann, Jim, Debbi, and Jonathan – this book is dedicated.

Introduction

Botswana is an African country with a small population. On both counts, the odds are low that it would persistently dominate the list of the world's fast-growing countries. Yet, for over three decades, Botswana's growth rate of gross domestic product (GDP) per capita outpaced that of the so-called Asian tigers. Other indicators, such as primary school enrolment and accumulation of foreign exchange reserves, also point to a development success story.

Why did per capita GDP grow so rapidly? Was this the result of luck or was it attributable to growth-promoting policies? On balance, I conclude that it was due to sound policies. But that still leaves the question: why those policies? The answer lies in a combination of the political system and the economic interests working within that system, tempered by tradition, institutions, and leadership. In looking at this combination I utilize the rational choice paradigm, which places heavy emphasis on the interests of individuals and their responses to incentives. Yet the roles of tradition, institutions, and leadership in shaping those rational choices are critical.

The people of Botswana live and work in a political system whose roots lie in both their own cultures and the British tradition. The interests of the elite, which dominated at Independence, have remained influential, leading some observers to suggest that Botswana is a democracy in name only. The evolution of economic and political institutions from the early post-Independence years influenced what Botswana has become. Leadership and ideas were also important. Thus, the political system and economic policies, both of which were modified over time, interacted to generate the path we now observe in retrospect. In other words, there is no single explanation for why Botswana prospered. Many influences, both simultaneous and varying, were at work.

My initial task is to trace the key elements of Botswana's growth story. I begin, in Chapter 1, by considering Botswana's economic and political record. I set out the overall economic growth, the structural transformation of the economy, and the booms and slumps experienced. The investment in physical and human capital, and the distribution of the income generated, are all important components of the growth story. Equally important is the story of Botswana's political development, starting from its foundations in Tswana history and moving through the British Protectorate and into the post-Independence evolution of a competitive democracy.

With the economic and political background in place, in Chapter 2 I set out the basic issues relating economic policies and democratic political systems to economic growth. This provides a framework within which to address the question of whether or not there is a relationship between Botswana's growth and its democracy. The stage is set with a brief review of the fundamentals underlying growth, followed by a review of the relationship between policy choice and interests in a democratic society. Because the evolution of institutions can have an important bearing on a nation's economic and political choices, I also look at the role of institutions.

In Chapter 3 I identify the forces shaping Botswana's policies since Independence. I start by looking at the baseline of interests at Independence and conclude by reviewing key elements in the post-Independence evolution of institutions, policies, and politics.

In Chapter 4 I interpret the evidence and offer an explanation for why Botswana prospered. The proximate explanation of Botswana's exceptional growth record has to do with its set of economic policies. Yet the choice and implementation of those policies were shaped by interests, institutions, and leadership that had strong roots in tribal society.

WHY BOTSWANA PROSPERED

1

Economic and Political Record

The headline numbers are striking: Botswana's real growth of GDP per capita, averaged over three and one-half decades, is the fastest in the world. But is the breadth and depth of the record of Botswana's economic, political, and social development equally striking? The record requires documentation. To provide an overall balanced picture, in Section 1 I offer a review of the economic record to date. It will become clear that not all indicators are equally bright. This leads me to offer a preliminary answer to the first question: is the Botswana record really exceptional? Despite a few negative dimensions, the answer remains yes.

In Section 2 I turn to the political record, tracing its foundations in tribal history through the establishment of an independent democracy to the present. This provides an answer to the second question: is Botswana truly a democracy? As with the first question, so with the second: despite a few negative features, the answer is yes.

1. THE ECONOMIC RECORD

Botswana's economic record includes not only growth of per capita GDP but also several measures of human and political development. Furthermore, Botswana is one of a very few countries that has been able to sustain high growth rates decade after decade.[1] Moreover, mineral-rich countries

Table 1.1
Botswana comparisons: Population, GDP per capita, and real growth of GDP
per capita to 1966–99

Country	1999 Population (thousands)	1999 GDP/Cap US $	11-Year Growth Rate (%)	22-Year Growth Rate (%)	33-Year Growth Rate (%)
Botswana	1,610	3,124	4.0	5.1	7.0
Chile	15,020	4,505	5.2	3.5	2.1
China	1,266,840	782	8.0	na	na
Hong Kong	6,840	23,247	1.8	3.9	4.6
Indonesia	209,260	654	2.7	3.1	3.8
Ireland*	3,750	19,644	5.9	4.2	4.1
Korea	46,860	8,684	5.1	5.7	6.1
Lesotho	2,110	437	2.5	na	na
Malaysia	22,710	3,467	4.4	na	na
Singapore	3,890	21,837	4.8	5.0	6.2
Thailand	61,810	2,006	4.4	4.7	4.6
Trinidad & T*	1,290	4,701	1.3	−0.1	1.1

Source: IMF, *International Financial Statistics.*
Notes: US $ GDP per capita calculated current price GDP, converted at average
exchange rate for 1999. Botswana GDP data are for national account years ending
30 June.
* Latest year for GDP data is 1998, hence growth rates are 10-year, 21-year, and
  32-year to 1998.

have seldom been able to accomplish such a feat.[2] The purpose of this section is to review the record – both the accom-
plishments and the disappointments – in order to provide
a setting within which to evaluate Botswana's policies.

Real Growth

In Table 1.1 Botswana's real GDP per capita growth over the
third of a century following Independence in 1966 is compared with a few other small countries and the larger fast-
growing economies of the world. It is particularly noticeable
that, over this entire period, there is *no* country with a faster
growth rate of GDP per capita than Botswana's. While some
countries have had higher growth rates than Botswana over
the most recent decade, not even the Asian tigers of Korea,
Thailand, and Singapore exceeded Botswana's rate for the

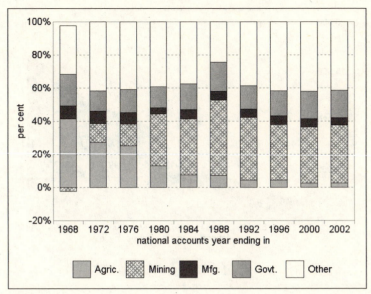

Figure 1.1
Shares of GDP
Sources:
a. Botswana Central Statistics Office, National Accounts of Botswana 1971–72, for national account years 1967/68 and 1971/72.
b. Botswana Central Statistics Office, National Accounts of Botswana, for subsequent years.

thirty-three years between 1966 and 1999. Another way of looking at Botswana's accomplishment is to say that, since Independence, its per capita GDP has moved from that of today's Mali to that of today's South Africa.

Structural Transformation[3]

The growth of the Botswana economy was accompanied by a dramatic transformation of the structure of economic activity. Figure 1.1 shows the distribution of nominal GDP at four-year intervals. At Independence, agriculture had been the largest single sector.[4] But the mineral sector, consisting mostly of diamonds plus copper-nickel, grew much more rapidly than did agriculture, making it the largest sector by the end of the 1970s. Government also played an

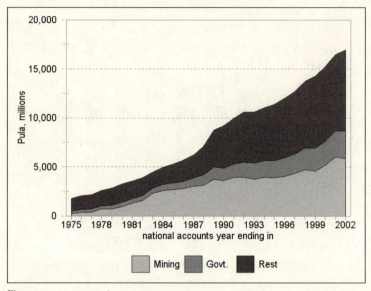

Figure 1.2
Real GDP by Major Sector: constant 1993/94 prices
Source: Botswana Central Statistics Office, National Accounts of Botswana.

increasing role in the economy not only measured as a producing sector but also as government expenditure relative
to GDP.

The growth of the Botswana economy was not simply a
story of a mineral enclave with an ever-growing government
attached to a stagnating traditional economy. This may be
seen more clearly in Figure 1.2, where the levels of the mineral
sector, the government sector, and the rest of the economy are
shown in constant 1993/94 prices. It is clear that the rest of
the economy experienced considerable real growth and that
real growth has been sustained even as the growth of the
mineral sector and the government sector has slackened.

Booms and Slumps

It is not unusual for an economy heavily dependent on one
mineral export to experience booms and dramatic slumps.[5]
If we look at individual sectors in Botswana, such a pattern

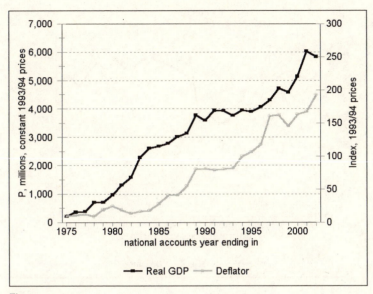

Figure 1.3
Mining
Source: calculated from Botswana Central Statistics Office, National Accounts of
Botswana.

emerges. Botswana's mineral sector has exhibited some substantial year-to-year changes (see Figure 1.3). Rapid growth
occurred in the early 1980s as a major new diamond mine
came on stream, but the world recession led to a drop in
the implicit sectoral deflator (mostly diamonds and copper
nickel). As the world economy boomed in the late 1980s
the implicit deflator rose dramatically, again to be followed
by a flat period and another boom and slump in the 1990s.

The high variance of the weather produced equally dramatic variation of real agricultural output (see Figure 1.4).
The drought of the early 1980s cut agricultural output by
about one-third, while the good rains of 1987/88 brought
a dramatic recovery.

Botswana had to contend with more than real shocks
hitting the output of two major producing sectors. The
international terms of trade exhibited dramatic year-to-year
changes (see Figure 1.5). Both wide swings and sharp year-

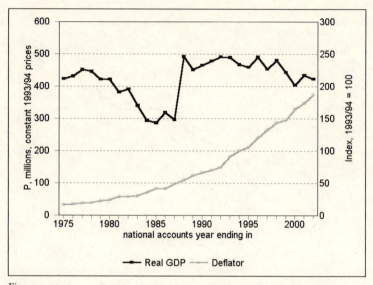

Figure 1.4
Agriculture
Source: calculated from Botswana Central Statistics Office, National Accounts of
Botswana.

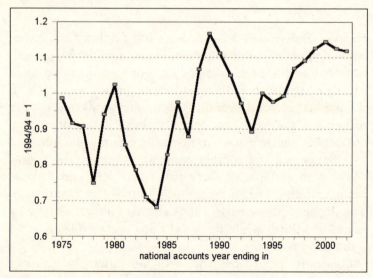

Figure 1.5
Terms of International Trade: Index
Source: calculated from Botswana Central Statistics Office, National Accounts of
Botswana.

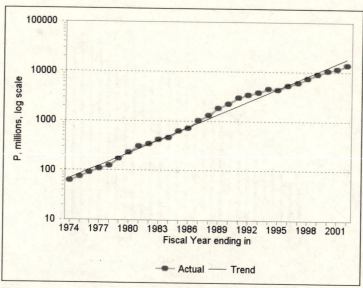

Figure 1.6
Government Expenditure and Net Lending
Source: Botswana Government, *Financial Statements, Tables and Estimates of the Consolidated and Development Fund Revenues.*

to-year changes in the terms of trade have had a substantial impact on the real income of such an open economy. Occasionally, the terms of trade would remain roughly the same as they were in the previous year; however, more often than not, dramatic changes would occur, averaging nearly 10% annually.

Government, however, was not a source of economic instability. This may be gauged by looking at nominal government expenditure plus net lending as a measure of government's overall impact on the economy (see Figure 1.6).[6] The scale is a log scale, so a constant nominal growth rate is represented by a straight line. The actual nominal series is shown by the dots, while the trend is shown by the solid line.

Government generally succeeded in avoiding extreme episodes of government-led inflation but was not always successful in keeping its expenditure and net lending on a steady growth path, particularly in the late 1980s and early

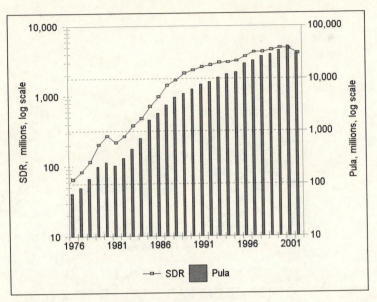

Figure 1.7
Foreign Exchange Reserves: calendar year end
Sources: Bank of Botswana, *Tenth Anniversary, 1975-1985*, for 1976 to 1981; *Annual Report 1993*, for 1982 to 1989; *Botswana Financial Statistics*, for 1990 to 2002.

1990s.[7] In the period from 1988/89 through 1991/92 government expenditure and net lending grew at well above the trend, resulting in Botswana's inflation exceeding that of its largest trading partner, South Africa, for the calendar years 1992 through 1994. The growth of government spending was finally reined in during 1994/95 by constraining the lending to parastatals.[8]

To accomplish a steady growth path for government expenditure and net lending, government savings – invested largely in foreign exchange reserves – served as a shock-absorber. It is clear in Figure 1.7 that this was particularly important in the early 1980s, when weakness in the diamond market resulted in no sales of diamonds for about half a year, forcing the country to dip into its foreign exchange reserves. On the upside, the rapid improvement in the diamond market in the later part of the 1980s and again in the mid-1990s accelerated the growth of the reserves.[9]

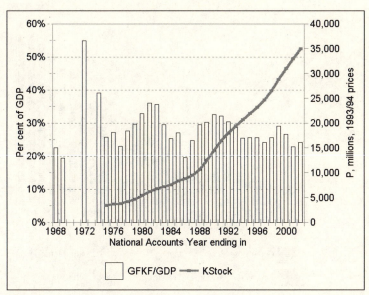

Figure 1.8
Gross Domestic Fixed Capital Formation and Capital Stock
Sources: Botswana Central Statistics Office, *National Accounts of Botswana 1974/75,*
for national account years 1967/68 to 1973/74; and *National Accounts of Botswana,*
for subsequent years.

Capital Investment

A major portion of the Botswana's rapidly growing income
was invested (see Figure 1.8). But, in the early years,
Botswana's own resources were not enough to finance the
needed investment. Donors and direct foreign investors
financed basic infrastructure and initiated major mineral
projects, especially those pertaining to diamonds and copper-
nickel. After the initial surge of investments, which were
huge relative to GDP, capital formation slowed somewhat.
Investment relative to GDP has tended to exhibit a cyclical
pattern, but the average level has continued to be high, similar to those of some of the rapidly growing countries of Asia
such as Malaysia and Thailand.
    Starting from practically zero, investment has succeeded
in building an impressive infrastructure in Botswana. This

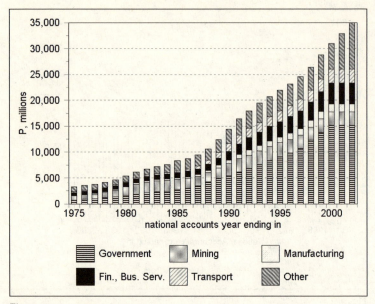

Figure 1.9
Capital Stock Composition: constant 1993/94 prices
Source: Botswana Central Statistics Office, *National Accounts of Botswana.*

includes not only the mines but also a substantial stock of modern-sector housing, tarred roads to virtually all parts of the country, an electricity generation and distribution system, a telephone system, dams and distribution of water, and schools and health clinics. Practically none of this was in existence at the time of Independence. The resulting capital stock series, in constant 1993/94 prices and broken down by major sector, is shown in Figure 1.9. What is noteworthy is the fact that in 1975 the government and the mining sector's capital stock were about equal, with each at about one-quarter of the total, while in 2000 government had doubled its share of the total to nearly 50%, and the mining sector's share had dropped to 8% of the total.

Population

The population of Botswana grew rapidly in the years following the Second World War, but, as real incomes grew,

Table 1.2
Population and demographic indicators

Census year	1946	1964	1971	1981	1991	2001
Population (thousands)						
Male	147.5	264.5	272.5	443.1	634.4	778.9
Female	148.8	278.6	324.4	497.9	692.4	841.3
Non-Batswana	na	1.5	10.9	15.7	29.6	60.7
Total resident	296.3	544.6	607.8	956.7	1,356.4	1,680.9
Growth rate (%)	1.1	3.0	3.1	3.4	2.7	2.2
Age distribution (%)						
0–4			17.6	18.5	14.6	11.6
5–14			29.9	28.8	28.6	25.9
15–64			46.9	47.6	51.8	58.2
65+			5.6	5.1	4.9	5.3
Life expectancy at birth (years)						
Male			52.5	52.3	63.3	52.8
Female			58.6	59.7	67.1	59.0
Urban (%)	na	3.9	9.1	17.7	45.7	54.2

Sources: Bechuanaland Protectorate Government, Census 1946, and Census 1964.
NDP 8, tables 1.1 and 1.2 for 1971, 1981, 1991, and 1997.
CSO, Stats Update, for 2001.
Notes: Age distribution groups reported in the 1946 and 1964 censuses do not correspond to the later censuses.
The 1946 and 1964 censuses did not provide estimates of life expectancy.
Growth rate at 1946 is calculated as the rate since the 1936 census. All others are estimated as of the census date.

the population growth rate dropped (see Table 1.2). At the same time, the portion of the population aged 15 to 64 has grown, thus reducing the dependency ratio. Another important feature of the demographics was the substantial increase in the life expectancy at birth.[10] A further notable feature of the demographic data is rapid urbanization. Some of this is the consequence of the changing nature of large traditional villages such as Mochudi and Serowe. In each census a village with a population of 5,000 or greater, and with more than 75% of the workforce involved in non-agricultural activities, is classified as urban. According to this definition, by the time of the 1991 census, nearly all of the major villages had become urban.

Table 1.3
Education enrolments (thousands)

	1965	1970	1975	1980	1985	1990	1995	2001
Primary	66.1	83	116	172	224	284	319	327.6
Secondary	1.3	3.9	12.1	18.3	32.2	56.9	105	151.2*
University	0.1	0.14	0.47	0.93	1.77	3.68	5.5	11.2*

Sources: For 1975 through 1995, NDP 8, table 2.5; for 1965 and 1970, NDP 1973–78, tables 7.12, 7.17, and 7.28.
For 2001, CSO *Statistical Bulletin*, vol. 26, nos. 2 and 3 (September 2001, published April 2003), table 1.2.
Note: * refers to 2000.

Human Development

Botswana's record in human development is as substantial as is its record in economic development – with one important exception: HIV infection. Throughout the country, major emphasis has been placed on providing basic education and primary health care.

Primary school enrolment has gone from 66,100 in 1966 to 327,600 in 2000, representing an average compound growth rate of 4.8% per annum (see Table 1.3). Further, in recent decades the gender balance has consistently reflected greater than 50% female enrolment. Meanwhile, secondary school and university enrolments, which start from much lower bases than does primary school enrolment, both grew at double digit rates. The gender balance in secondary schooling also favours females.

High primary school enrolment rates over extended periods have resulted in a substantial increase in the proportion of the population that has at least completed primary education (see Figure 1.10). From the 1964 census to the 2001 census the proportion of the population with completed primary education or better has moved from 1.5% to 43%. The fact that the proportion of the population with primary education did not grow faster reflects the success of the health system in improving the lifespan of those members of the older generation who had not had the benefit of primary education.

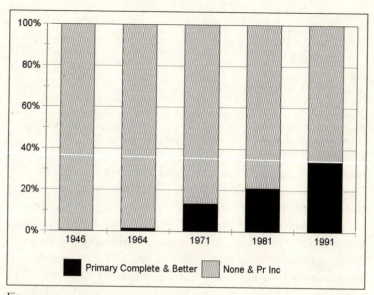

Figure 1.10
Educational Attainment: census years
Sources:
a. Bechuanaland Protectorate, *Census 1964*, for 1946 and 1964.
b. Botswana Central Statistics Office, *Census 1971, 1981, 1991*, and 2001 for subsequent years.

Since the mid-1970s the health care strategy has emphasized the widespread provision of primary health care to the many rather than the provision of hospitals and doctors to the few. Today, virtually all urban residents are within fifteen kilometres of a primary care facility, as are 83% of rural residents. The data on health services (see Table 1.4) show that, ever since 1980, the expansion of nurses (mostly in primary care clinics) exceeds that of doctors and hospital beds.[11] This approach to health care has resulted in a dramatic fall in infant mortality (from 100 per 1,000 live births in 1971 to forty-five in 1991) and, before accounting for the impact of AIDS, in an increase in life expectancy at birth (from less than fifty years at Independence to the upper sixties in the 1990s).

The exception to the success story in health has been the spread of HIV. A substantial portion of the sexually active

Table 1.4
Health services (per 100,000 population)

	1980	1985	1990	1995	2001
Doctors	15	17	18	27	28
Nurses	124	176	188	252	297
Hospital beds	226	235	247	230	218

Sources: NDP 8, table 2.5 for 1980; and CSO Statistical Bulletin, vol. 26, nos. 2 and 3 (September 2001, published April 2003) for subsequent years.

population – more than one-third – is now HIV positive.[12] Despite over a decade of active advertising campaigns and the widespread cheap/free distribution of condoms, behaviour did not change and transmission of HIV accelerated throughout Botswana. The impact of this on the population's morbidity and death rate is not yet fully estimated. However, it will certainly reverse much of the success in increasing the life expectancy noted above,[13] and it will bring misery to a large part of the population in the coming years.

Various plans announced in 2000 and 2001 with regard to HIV/AIDS care and prevention, including a substantial donation of US$100 million from the Bill and Melinda Gates Foundation along with the involvement of major international drug companies, hold out some promise for an eventual turning of the corner. But the long lag from a change in behaviour to a change in incidence of HIV means that the impact of existing infection rates will continue to affect society for many years.[14]

The impact of HIV on the economy does not parallel the misery associated with it. The growth rate of output will be reduced by perhaps 1% per annum, as will the growth rate of the population, leaving those who survive with roughly the same GDP per capita as they would have had without the AIDS effect.[15]

Unemployment

The rapid population growth experienced by Botswana in the early years after Independence generated an equally rapid growth in the labour force in the 1990s (estimated to be about 3.4% per annum). While there is no long-standing comprehensive labour force survey that is used to estimate the unemployment rate, data from the censuses and the 1993/94 Household Income and Expenditure Surveys (HIES) provide numbers which suggest a serious and growing unemployment problem in the early 1990s. The 1991 census reported an unemployment rate of 14%, and the 1993/94 HIES reported a rate of 21%.[16]

Income Distribution

The national development plans have long proclaimed social justice as one of their four planning objectives.[17] To the extent that this involves reducing income inequality, the success has been modest. Income inequality in Botswana, by international standards, is high but not exceptionally high. One measure of income inequality is the Gini coefficient, which ranges from zero (perfect equality) to one (complete inequality). Typically, a coefficient of 0.5 or greater is considered high. Data based on an adequate sample have been collected on three occasions in Botswana – 1974/75 for the rural population only (the Rural Income Distribution Survey [RIDS]), and in 1985/86 and again in 1993/94 for the entire population (HIES).[18] The results, summarized in Table 1.5, show that, while the income distribution in the rural areas has become more equal over time, there has been no change for the urban population.[19] For the nation as a whole, the Gini index of inequality barely declined from 1985/86 to 1993/94, and it remained in excess of 0.5. In other words, the rapid growth of real per capita GDP has scarcely touched the relative distribution of measured income. While the rich are better off than before, so are the poor.

The definition of income in the HIES includes non-cash income in kind, such as meals provided by an employer, consumption of one's own produce, or school meals. But the HIES does *not* reflect publicly provided education and health care. These services make up a substantially greater portion

Table 1.5
Gini coefficients for total income, Botswana

	RIDS, 1974/75	HIES, 1985/86	HIES, 1993/94
National		0.556	0.537
Urban		0.536	0.539
Urban villages			0.451
Rural	0.52	0.477	0.414

Sources: HIES 1993/94, 60; RIDS 1974/75, 85.

Table 1.6
Poverty rates, Botswana households (%)

	1985/86	1993/94
Very poor (< food requirement)	33	23
Poor (but > very poor)	16	15
Total poor	49	38

Source: BIDPA (1997), table 3.2.

of the true income of lower income households than of higher income households. Consequently, we can conclude that, if the Gini coefficients were corrected to include publicly provided education and health services, then there would be a significant reduction in measured income inequality.

The Gini coefficient does not measure poverty. For this, the data for the HIES must be combined with a poverty datum line (PDL) to identify the portion of the population that falls below such a line. The specification of a PDL is by no means uncontroversial, and Botswana's PDL[20] is no exception. In light of this, BIDPA (1997) distinguished between poor (those below the PDL) and very poor (those with an income below the food requirement in the PDL). This also approximates the commonly used international cut-off of one dollar a day (at 1985 prices and exchange rates) to identify the very poor. The proportion of households identified as very poor declined over the period from 1985/86 to 1993/94 (Table 1.6), while the proportion between the Central Statistics Office (CSO) PDL and the basic food requirement has remained roughly constant.

A related issue concerns the income gap between the rural and urban areas. In 1993/94 the average monthly income (cash and non-cash) of households headed by citizens in rural areas was half that of those in urban areas.[21] The 1985/86 HIES does not have exactly the same breakdown, but the ratio is approximately the same.[22] It is noteworthy that the measured rural-urban disposable income difference has persisted even though, as we saw in Table 1.2, there has been a massive shift of the population from rural to urban. Again, the fact that the data exclude publicly provided health care and education suggests some caution. The provision of these services began initially in the urban areas and gradually spread to the rural areas. In other words, the true rural-urban income gap has almost certainly narrowed.

2. POLITICAL DEVELOPMENT

Botswana's modern political system evolved both from the traditional Tswana culture and the British tradition introduced during the Protectorate. The particulars of the mix, however, were by no means predetermined.

Foundations in Tswana History

During the centuries prior to the establishment of the Bechuanaland Protectorate in 1885, aggressive expansion by both black and white neighbours from the south had dispersed the Tswana tribes[23] over a wide area, including much of what is now Botswana.[24] Two features profoundly shaped the response of the Tswana people: the abundance of land and the mobility of the principal capital asset, cattle. Together, these meant that it was relatively easy to move on rather than to fight to retain control over a specific territory. The exit option applied not only to the tribe as a whole but also to subgroups.[25] The result was a dispersion of geographically separated groups, with a common language and institutions, reflecting a common heritage.

The Tswana settler colonies, much as the European settler colonies elsewhere in Africa, needed a modicum of
public goods such as law and order, defence against raiders,
and public works. These services were provided through
the adaptation of Tswana traditions. Every tribe had "age
regiments," consisting of cohorts of similar aged individuals who had been initiated together as youths in separate
male and female regiments. When summoned by the chief,
an age regiment was required to perform duties for the
common good.[26]

The role and power of the chiefs were profoundly influenced by the ease of exit. To persuade the tribal members
to accept the chief's leadership for the common good,
including the provision of public goods via the age regiments, an implicit bargain between the chief and his people
emerged. The chief provided leadership, but the people
required accountability.

Schapera (1953, 46), an early anthropological authority
on the Tswana, describes the chief's duties in the following
terms: "He was expected to watch over the interests of his
subjects, and keep informed of tribal affairs generally; he
therefore spent much time daily at his *kgotla* (council-
place), where anybody could approach him directly with
news, petitions, and complaints ... If his own conduct was
unsatisfactory, he could be warned or reprimanded by his
advisers or at public assemblies; if he ruled despotically or
repeatedly neglected his duties, the people would begin to
desert him, or a more popular relative would try to oust
him by force."

Schapera goes on to describe the traditional tribal meeting:

All matters of public policy are dealt with finally at an assembly
open to all men of the tribe. ... Such assemblies are held very
frequently, at times weekly, and they usually meet early in the
morning in the tribal council-place, close to the chief's residence.
Normally only the men present in the capital attend, the business
discussed and decisions reached being communicated, if necessary,
to the inhabitants of outlying villages through their headmen. But

on important occasions the men from outside are also summoned ... Since anybody present is entitled to speak, the tribal assemblies provide a ready means of ascertaining public opinion ... The discussions are characterized by considerable freedom of speech, and if the occasion seems to call for it, the chief or his advisers may even be severely criticized. (47).

The chief served as judge in both criminal and civil matters but was not free to make up the rules of the game. In other words, the chief was not above the law of the tribe; rather, as Crowder, Parsons, and Parsons (1990, 10) characterise it, there is "a strong sense of constitutionalism." It is summed up by the admonition given a new ruler at his installation: "The king is king by the grace of the people."[27] Where the chief had to arbitrate between members or groups, great value was placed on achieving a compromise with which all could live, while not triggering an exit by a disgruntled minority.

A further consequence of the ease of exit was that no single Tswana state dominated its neighbours. Each of the major tribes was relatively autonomous, having chosen its new location to ensure that it would not be dominated as it was difficult to maintain control over great distances. The high variance of the climate, and the ongoing threat of aggression from both white and black neighbours, placed a premium on cooperation among the Tswana tribes. But intertribal cooperation and resolution of disputes had to be negotiated rather than dictated by a dominant individual or tribe.[28] Such cooperation was not always forthcoming. To this day, some adjacent tribes exhibit more hostility than neighbourliness towards each other.

Not all Tswana settler colonies had migrated into uninhabited land. Some, particularly those covering large geographical areas in the northern part of today's Botswana, had moved to lands where other non-Tswana tribes were already present. There thus began a process of administrative and cultural assimilation of the non-Tswana groups.[29]

The harsh climate had an important effect on shaping attitudes towards good times and bad. The value of saving during times of plenty, and sharing during times of drought, profoundly shaped Tswana attitudes well beyond Independence.

In each Tswana polity the elite was firmly in charge of both tribal politics and the economy. The chief was assisted in his duties by counsellors and, in villages outside the principal one, by headmen. Land was held by the tribe and allocated by the chief. By tradition, each family was entitled to allocations for a home, for crops, and for grazing.[30] Since the principal private asset was cattle, owners of large cattle herds were the effective economic elite. This elite had a clear interest in maintaining property rights, and did so.[31]

The elite also had an interest in education. As Engerman and Sokoloff (1997) point out, educated people represented a scarce resource. Since, initially, public education was not provided, only the elite could afford to invest in education. Moreover, education was recognized as necessary to deal with both the British and the traders. Illustrative of this was Tshekedi Khama's insistence, while he was Bamangwato regent, that his nephew and heir, Seretse Khama, be sent to Britain to receive an academic education rather than to Rhodesia to learn a trade.

In brief, the Tswana settler colonies, much like the European settler colonies elsewhere in the world, retained a continuity with their traditions and institutions.

British Protectorate

In 1885 much of the territory of modern Botswana was established as the Bechuanaland Protectorate, not a Crown colony. In light of the circumstances of the day, this minimalist arrangement suited both the British and the Tswana chiefs. Botswana did not have the rich agricultural lands sought by European settlers elsewhere in Africa (e.g., Kenya). There were few known natural resources (such as those found in the Gold Coast) worth exploiting. But, given the existence of minerals in the region, the potential for finding such resources did exist.[32] At the same time, the mobility of the economy's principal capital asset – cattle – meant that a government's ability to engage in predatory taxation would be substantially limited. Hence the imperial power had little incentive to establish firm control over Botswana's economy. By some accounts, the Protectorate arrangement had been sought by at least one of the Tswana chiefs.[33] Certainly such an arrangement brought mutual benefit to both the Tswana chiefs and the British government. So far as the latter was concerned, the Protectorate device thwarted the advances of the Germans from the west and the Boers from the east, at minimal out-of-pocket cost to the British. As for the Tswana chiefs, the loss of effective power was minimal, at least in the initial stages: the British were to protect the territory from external aggression, while the chiefs were to govern internally "in their own fashion."[34]

In the early 1890s, the territory of the Protectorate was extended northward to include all of modern-day Botswana. Further, the British unilaterally extended the power of the high commissioner for South Africa to include executive and legislative powers in the Protectorate, primarily as those powers affected whites.

The Bechuanaland Protectorate included a natural corridor between British controlled Cape Colony in South Africa and the future Rhodesia. In 1895, when it appeared that the British South Africa Company, led by Cecil Rhodes, wished to extend its influence into the Protectorate, a remarkable coalition of Tswana chiefs and British missionary interests succeeded in mounting an effective counter campaign in Britain (see Parsons 1998). However, not all Tswana tribes were successful in escaping the advances from the southeast. Well over half of today's Tswana speakers are South African as they resided in territory that was outside the Protectorate and that, in 1909, became part of the Union of South Africa.

The Protectorate remained a backwater for the British well into the second half of the twentieth century. The role of governor was carried by the British high commissioner to the Union of South Africa, who doubled as high commissioner for the three territories of Bechuanaland, Basotholand, and Swaziland, collectively labelled the "High Commission Territories."[35] In each there was a resident commissioner. However, in the case of the Bechuanaland Protectorate, he was not actually resident in the territory as the administrative capital was in Mafeking, South Africa.

The British continued the policy of leaving the chiefs to govern internally, and they reinforced the authority of these chiefs (by force, if necessary). The identification of a specific geographic territory with each tribe gradually came to mean that each Tswana chief gained jurisdiction over all residents of his territories.[36] The exit option was no longer there for the taking. Thus both subordinate Tswana and non-Tswana became subject to the authority of the Tswana chief who presided over their particular tribal territory. Since there was no geographic territory for non-Tswana tribes, this system led to the cultural dominance of the Tswana. Some, such as the Kalanga, resented and resisted this attempt at cultural assimilation.[37] While the chief, once appointed, had considerable power within his tribal territory, the British remained ready to remove him should they deem him unacceptable.[38]

Government services were provided through a combination of tribal and Protectorate initiative. In the absence of any budgetary transfers from Britain, both had to be financed from local sources.[39] Given the very limited tax base, services were consequently minimal. The result was that "government services [fell] far below an acceptable level for a territory administered by imperial Britain."[40]

Change in the political arrangements for the Protectorate was slow to develop. From the time of the 1909 British parliamentary act that established the Union of South Africa, both the British and the South African governments believed that some day the three High Commission Territories would be incorporated into South Africa. Despite the opposition of the tribal chiefs, this view persisted well into the post-Second World War period. However, following the 1948 victory of the National Party in South Africa, with its increasing emphasis on apartheid, the British gradually

Table 1.7
Bechuanaland Protectorate Government revenues and expenditures (£,000)

Year end	Expend.	Revenue	Grant in aid	Balance	Grant/exp (%)
1957	1,230.7	992.8	140.0	(97.9)	11.4
1958	1,633.7	967.4	480.0	(186.3)	29.4
1959	1,612.9	1,125.3	560.0	72.4	34.7
1960	1,912.8	1,237.2	650.0	(25.6)	34.0
1961	2,270.6	1,283.7	970.0	(16.9)	42.7
1962	2,881.5	1,641.9	1,155.0	(84.6)	40.1
1963	2,706.8	1,578.5	1,128.0	(0.3)	41.7
1964	3,142.0	1,848.3	1,293.7	0.0	41.2
1965	3,258.4	2,123.3	1,126.1	(9.0)	34.6
1966	3,413.5	2,385.0	1,028.5	0.0	30.1
1967	3,556.4	2,587.5	968.9	(0.0)	27.2
1968	3,699.8	2,783.0	916.8	(0.0)	24.8

Source: Bechuanaland Protectorate, Development Plan 1963/68, table 1, p. 45.
Notes: 1957 to 1962 are actual; 1963 is approved estimate; 1964+ are projected.

came to recognize that such an option would not be acceptable internationally.[41] Thus, in the second half of the 1950s,
the British began to contemplate new political arrangements
for the Protectorate. At roughly the same time, it began to
provide modest budgetary assistance to the Protectorate,
permitting a small expansion of government services. In the
1956/57 fiscal year, the British "grant-in-aid" amounted to
£140,000 and covered 11% of the Protectorate Government's expenditure. By the 1960/61 fiscal year the share
covered by Britain had jumped to over 40%, which is where
it remained for several years (Table 1.7).

The path of political change was significantly influenced
by personalities. The largest single Tswana tribe was the
Bamangwato. Chief Khama III had been instrumental in
the original approach to establishing the British Protectorate in 1885 and in the campaign to block Rhodes' expansion. From 1925 the Bamangwato had been led by a regent,
Tshekedi Khama, awaiting the coming of age and education
of his nephew, Seretse Khama. Tshekedi had a forceful per-
sonality and was widely acknowledged as the leading
spokesperson for all the chiefs of the Protectorate. In 1948

the British had objected to the marriage between Seretse Khama and Ruth Williams (a white Englishwoman) and banned Seretse from returning to the Protectorate. Tshekedi also objected to the marriage. The matter was discussed in the Bamangwato *kgotla* on three occasions, and in June 1949 most of the tribe endorsed the marriage. Feeling rejected, Tshekedi left the tribal territory. After Seretse's exile of several years, in 1956 Tshekedi met with him in England. They both agreed to renounce their respective claims to the chieftaincy and to return to their Ngwato tribal territory to work towards the creation of a tribal council, thus effectively formalizing the tribe's democratic constraints on the chief.

There began a decade of constitutional changes, both at the tribal and the Protectorate levels. The Ngwato Tribal Council was instituted, with both Tshekedi and Seretse Khama being heavily involved. This model was soon generalized and extended to other tribes. The advisory councils, which had been introduced after the First World War, were increasingly involved in debating and approving proposed legislation. In 1958 the advisory councils asked for the creation of a legislative council. This led to an extensive consultative process that, in 1961, generated a transitional constitution that lasted until self-government in 1965. The process of negotiating the new dispensation and the subsequent functioning of the representative legislature and the executive were described by the resident commissioner, the British representative on the ground at the time, as "decision making by consensus."[42]

One of the early tasks of the new Protectorate Government was the preparation of a request for grants from Britain for the five year period between 1963 and 1968. Since Britain was providing over 40% of government expenditures (see Table 1.7), it was crucial to put forward a convincing case. The plan was drawn up during an extensive consultative process that involved not only British officials but also members of the executive and the legislature. The resultant document, Bechuanaland Protectorate, *Development Plans*

1963/1968, set out in some detail the basic information about the country, its people, its physical and human resources, its economy, and its administrative and political background. It then went on to state the key policies and priorities, and to discuss how they would be financed, before listing and costing (to the last pound) the various development schemes. This early exercise in consultation over expenditure priorities and plans covering a multi-year time period was in keeping with the *kgotla* tradition of consultation and compromise; therefore, the post-Independence government adopted it as its mode of operation.

At the same time, political parties began to emerge. A relatively radical group established the People's Party (BPP)[43] in 1960, proposing immediate independence and abolition of the chieftaincy. In 1962 Seretse Khama took a leading role in founding the Democratic Party (BDP), a rural-based party that was more respectful of traditions than was the BPP.

The 1961 constitution was transitional. With a wave of independence sweeping over Africa, the British government made it clear that it wished to take the next steps. After announcing its intention in 1962, Britain held a constitutional conference in mid-1963, which led to a white paper on internal self-government. That constitution, in turn, formed the backbone of the Independence constitution (Fawcus and Tilbury 2000).

Two key features of the new constitution were (1) the election of the legislature (National Assembly) by a system of one-person, one-vote (applicable to all races)[44] and (2) the creation of a House of Chiefs. The role and composition of the House of Chiefs reflects a balancing of various interests at the time of the constitutional discussions. Its role is limited to the provision of advice on tribal and customary matters. For example, all bills dealing with tribal matters had to be referred to the House of Chiefs, but the National Assembly could ignore its advice in passing a law. In other words, the House of Chiefs has no veto. For many, the lack of legislative power suggested that the House of Chiefs was largely irrelevant and not worth fighting over. This made it relatively easy to entrench the dominance of the Tswana. Eight designated Tswana tribes, corresponding to eight geographic districts, were granted permanent seats, while the four remaining districts were each represented by one of the chiefs from those districts (in addition to three named by the president). With representation in the House of Chiefs, any chief wishing to be elected to the legislature had to resign his chieftaincy.[45]

Parallel with the discussion of the new constitutional arrangements, the British initiated a discussion on the reform of local government arrangements. This led to elected district councils with responsibility for local government both in the new urban areas and in the tribal areas (which had been governed by chiefs). This left the chiefs with limited customary functions; critically, however, they retained responsibility for presiding over the *kgotla* in their tribal seats. For a few years the chiefs also retained responsibility for land allocation in the tribal territories. In 1970, however, this responsibility was transferred to government-appointed tribal land boards. Thus, the process of replacing multi-tribal polities with a single national polity was begun gradually. And it was undoubtedly made easier by the fact that there was no single "paramount chief" with a legitimate claim to national power.

The constitution for internal self-government came into force in 1965. The arrangements fitted well with both the British parliamentary tradition, (Cabinet accountable to Parliament, along with a permanent civil service), and with the Tswana *kgotla* tradition of reaching consensus through open debate. In the elections of that year Seretse Khama's BDP won twenty-eight seats while the BPP garnered only three. Khama thus became prime minister and then president of the new Republic of Botswana at Independence in 1966.

Ethnic Composition

By the time the Bechuanaland Protectorate was established, the Tswana chiefs were clearly dominant over much of what

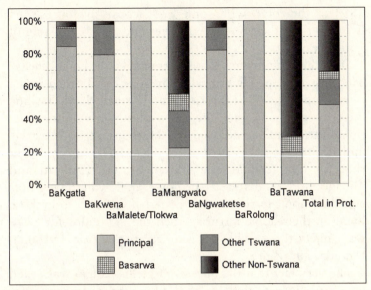

Figure 1.11
Ethnic Distribution of Population: 1946 census
Source: Bechuanaland Protectorate, *Census 1946.*

is now Botswana. Their dominance was reinforced by the British Protectorate's "indirect rule" approach, which gave the Tswana chiefs primacy in their tribal territories. However, the various Tswana tribes were not the only ethnic groups in the territory: several distinct non-Tswana groups constituted significant minorities.

The only systematic collection of data on ethnic composition throughout the Protectorate was carried out as part of the 1946 census.[46] At that time, the "population of the principal and allied tribes" in each of the tribal territories was tabulated. The disparity across the different tribal territories is quite striking (see Figure 1.11).[47] In some of the smaller tribal territories no minorities were reported, whereas in the largest territory, the home of Khama's Bamangwato, only 20% were Bamangwato, 21% were other Tswana, and nearly 60% were various non-Tswana, including 9.5% classified as "MaSarwa" (San, or bushmen).[48] In the Protectorate as a whole, including the freehold lands and towns, Tswana living in their own territories comprised

48% of the total, with some 16% consisting of Tswana living outside their home territories and 36% consisting of non-Tswana.[49]

Does this ethnic composition represent ethnic homogeneity? The answer depends crucially on how the Tswana living outside their home territories are classified. If all Tswana are treated as one, then the index of ethno-linguistic fractionalization (ELF) employed by Mauro (1995) and Easterly and Levine (1997) is in the low fifties. This is similar to that for Switzerland, the United States, Trinidad and Tobago, and Zimbabwe.[50] If, however, Tswana living outside their home territories are treated as different from those living in their home territory, then the ELF index for 1946 was ninety-three, which is similar to that for Tanzania, Uganda, and Zaire.

The very fact that the question of tribal origin was asked in 1946 suggests that, at that time, the distinction was important to some authority and very likely reflected the de facto tribal distinctions felt by the people. It is noteworthy that, in subsequent censuses, the question was proscribed, reflecting the emphasis placed on national unity from the run-up to Independence onwards.

The Republic at Independence

The political forces in the newly independent Republic of Botswana displayed a fundamental continuity with the traditional society of the previous century. Respect for the traditional leadership of the chieftaincy was now focused on the president but principally as a presiding officer rather than as a *caudillo*. The political elite and the economic elite remained coincident, much as a century before, with interests centred on ownership of cattle. The virtue of compromise continued to be firmly embedded in the political culture. This continuity with tradition stood in sharp contrast to the situation that prevailed in many other African countries at independence. All too often independence elections simply resulted in a winner-take-all situation.

Yet enormous changes were required in Botswana. A modern government apparatus had to be constructed, both institutionally and physically. The nature and functioning of Parliament, the Cabinet, and the civil service had to be settled. These new institutions drew heavily on the experience of the previous decade, moving from advisory councils to legislative and executive councils, and eventually to an elected internal form of self-government. Various government services, ranging from education to health to roads to finance, had to be established. The physical capital city, including government buildings and housing for government officers, was still under construction.

Political Competition: Elections, 1965–99

The post-independence institutional and policy evolution took place within a governance system that subjected itself to regular parliamentary and local council elections. The elections themselves met the usual international tests of "free and fair." What is of interest, then, is the outcome of these elections.

The pre-independence elections of 1965 had produced an overwhelming victory for the BDP, led by Seretse Khama, with 80% of the popular vote and the capturing of twenty-eight of the thirty-one seats in the legislature (see Figure 1.12a). This firmly established the BDP as the dominant party, with strong roots in the largely rural traditional society. The principal opposition party at the time was the BPP, described by Fawcus and Tilbury (2000, 90) as "radical, forceful and articulate." It won two seats in the second urban centre, Francistown, and a third in Mochudi, a large village and tribal seat near Gaborone.[51] The pattern for subsequent elections was thus set, with the BDP dominant in the rural constituencies and the BPP's principal strength being in certain urban areas.

The first post-independence elections were held in 1969. Thereafter, elections have been held every five years. Prior to the 1969 election, a new opposition party, the Botswana

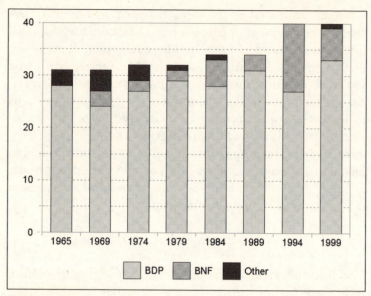

Figure 1.12a
Election Results, Seats: 1965–1999

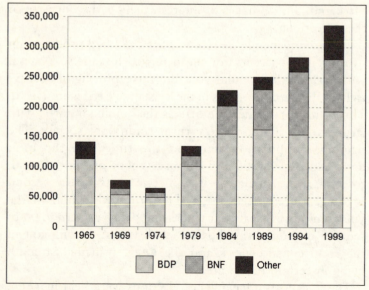

Figure 1.12b
Election Results, Votes; 1965–1999
Sources:

a. Botswana Independent Electoral Commission, 1999, *Report...*, for 1999.
b. Baummogger, 1999, for earlier years.

National Front (BNF), emerged at the initiative of Kenneth Koma.[52] On the basis of a platform that attempted to draw together both disaffected chiefs and radicals of the political left, the BNF was able to edge out the BPP for the second position in the popular vote, while the BDP slipped to 68% of the popular vote.

In every election since 1969, the BDP maintained an absolute majority of the popular vote and the bulk of the seats, while the BNF has continued in second place (see Figure 1.12b). Over the years, the various opposition parties have suffered from internal disputes, which, under the first-past-the-post system, impaired their ability to capture more than a few seats in the National Assembly.

For its part, the BDP, aware of the advantages of incumbency, was generally able to maintain internal discipline. An orderly succession, both in the party and the government, occurred in 1980 with the death of Seretse Khama. Vice-President Quett Ketumile Masire, who had been founding secretary general of the BDP, and who had carried the Cabinet post of minister of finance (and, later, development planning), succeeded to the office of president. Nevertheless, as agriculture shrank to less than 5% of GDP in the 1980s and the structure of the economy changed, the BDP's rural power base gradually eroded. By the 1994 election, the BDP's vote share slipped to just under 55%, and the opposition BNF captured thirteen seats, principally in the rapidly growing urban centres.

The new strength of the opposition produced dissension not only in the BDP but also in the opposition parties. The BDP and Masire attempted to solve the problem in early 1998 by renewing the leadership. Masire retired, passing the party leadership and the presidency to his vice-president, Festus Mogae. In turn, Ian Khama, eldest son of Seretse Khama, retired as commander of the Botswana Defence Force. A sitting member of Parliament in Serowe (the Bamangwato tribal seat) vacated the seat, which Khama won easily in a bye-election. Mogae appointed Khama as vice-president.

The opposition parties failed to take advantage of the BDP's shrinking power base. In the lead up to the 1999 elections, several BNF members of the National Assembly split from Koma to form a new party, the Botswana Congress party (BCP). The BCP took over most of the BNF seats in Parliament and became the official opposition. But the new party was routed in the 1999 elections and lost most of its seats. The BNF was restored to the official opposition, but with significantly fewer seats than it had won in 1994.[53] The 1999 election results thus reversed the downward slide of the BDP's share of the popular vote and seats in the National Assembly. The BDP captured 57% of the vote but a substantially greater share of the seats (thirty-three out of forty).

Indicators of Democracy

Various sources provide information on the state of democratic freedoms in Botswana relative to a broad range of countries throughout the world. A widely cited index prepared by the American organization Freedom House[54] has reported indices of political rights and of civil liberties since the early 1970s. On both scales Botswana has been assigned an index of two, on a scale ranging from one (most freedom) to seven (least freedom). Without explicitly stating the reasons for a rating of less than one, the latest report notes limited access to government-controlled broadcast media, concern over treatment of the San people, limitations on workers' right to strike, and slow progress on women's rights. On each of these, Botswana does not match the Western ideal of democracy. At the same time, Botswana has not been listed in Amnesty International's annual publication pertaining to countries who engage in egregious practices.[55]

A somewhat different, but obviously related, dimension is captured by Transparency International in its "corruption perceptions index." In its 2003 report Botswana was assigned an index of 5.7 on a scale that ranges from zero to ten, with ten being the least corrupt.[56] Botswana is ranked equal to Taiwan, better than Italy and Malaysia, and slightly lower than Belgium. In addition, a local chapter of Transparency International was established in Botswana in early 2001, and it published a review of policies, laws, and regulations aimed at combating corruption (Briscoe and Hermans 2001). Later that year the Botswana Society (a broadly based "learned society" that sponsors and publishes works on Botswana) held a symposium on the issue.

Nature of Botswana's Governance

Botswana's governance since Independence is widely cited as democratic, and many point to the roots of that democracy in the traditional Tswana culture. While there is broad agreement as to the key features of democracy in the Western world, and general agreement as to the nature of Tswana traditions, there is considerable debate about the nature and source of Botswana's democracy.

The multi-country study *Democracy in Developing Countries* (Diamond, Linz, and Lipset 1988) set out three essential characteristics of a democracy: (1) extensive competition; (2) inclusive political participation, with regular and fair elections; and (3) civil and political liberties. Crick (1989), the keynote speaker at a Botswana Society symposium on democracy in Botswana (Holm and Molutsi 1989), suggests that democracy in the Western world requires *both* power of the people and individual rights and liberties. Like Crick, duToit (1995) cites what he calls the standard procedural definition of democracy – selection of leaders through competitive elections – and adds the requirement that citizenship be of equal value to all when it comes to making claims against the state.

When these concepts are applied to modern Botswana, several indicators suggest a sturdy democracy. Free and fair parliamentary and local government elections have been regularly held, as prescribed by the Constitution. An active and articulate opposition has elected a significant number of members to Parliament in the elections of the 1990s. The opposition has also controlled several important local government councils, including the capital, for several years. A vigorous press routinely criticizes government actions. There was an orderly transition from the first to the second president (1980) and then from the second to the third president (1998). The judiciary has, on repeated occasions, brought government up short, declaring specific government actions illegal. Further, in such cases government has not proceeded to change the legislation or Constitution to legitimize its actions.[57] Finally, government has repeatedly been effective in preventing the transformation of droughts into famine.

Did today's democracy arise from Tswana custom, particularly the tradition of the chiefs' accountability to the people? Recall that the principal vehicle for accountability was the *kgotla*, or tribal meeting, in which all (male) members of the polity could, and often would, express their opinions concerning important (or not so important) matters, such as the way in which tribal affairs were being administered. Whether or not this feature of Tswana culture should be termed democratic depends very much on one's perspective. Schapera (1953) notes that, while in traditional Tswana society women are excluded from the *kgotla*, they have also acted as regents during the minority of a chief.[58] Peters (1995), also an anthropologist, sees little in Tswana tradition as democratic, dismissing it on the grounds that it excluded women as well as such minorities as the San (bushmen).

Various assessments of Botswana's democracy were offered in the Botswana Society Symposium (Holm and Molutsi 1989). Numerous contributors identify democratic features of Botswana's system, while others point to significant shortcomings. L.D. Ngcongco, a historian, concludes that the traditional Tswana state had a democratic character. He cites its consultative nature and openness, and argues that the structure "taught the people the necessity of observing and participating in their own governance" (Ngcongco 1989, 47) Datta and Murray (1989), in the same volume, focus on the historical dimension of minority rights. They point out that, before Independence, all non-Tswana were "subject groups." Some, such as the Kalanga and the Tswapong, were politically, culturally, and economically similar to the Tswana, and were assimilated into Tswana society. However, those like the San, who were handicapped by the absence of Tswana-type headmen, lacked a permanent meeting place, and were racially distinct, remained outside Tswana cultural hegemony and are still denied basic political and economic rights. Thirty-five years after Independence, both of these issues – Tswana cultural hegemony and the rights of the San – continue to be the subject of intense debate in Botswana. Yet, if one accepts Crick's characterization of democracy, it is clear that Tswana tradition has important features in common with Western democracy.

Holm (1988), a political scientist and the author of the Botswana chapter in Diamond, Linz, and Lipset (1988), provides a comprehensive analysis of the historical context; the structure, functioning, and theoretical underpinnings of democracy; and a review of the potential for reversal of democracy in Botswana. Although he argues that traditional chiefly governance was highly authoritarian and not inherently democratic, he nevertheless acknowledges two significant constraints on the power of a traditional Tswana chief: first, the chief always had to face the potential that his relatives might usurp his authority; second, there was a widely held expectation that the chief would abide by traditional law. Both constraints remain strong forces in Botswana's political culture today.[59]

Holm also argues that there is an ethnic base to Botswana's politics. He cites the BDP's overwhelming support in the Central District, which coincides with Seretse Khama's Bamangwato tribal territory and is the largest single district (nearly 40% of the population at Independence). However, Holm fails to recognize the ethnic heterogeneity of the Bamangwato tribal territory, where, as is shown in Figure 1.11, the Bamangwato themselves represented only 20% of the district's population. This might more appropriately be cited as evidence of the Tswana cultural hegemony noted by Datta and Murray (1989). Holm further suggests that there is a nascent conflict between the political elite and the bureaucracy but that democratic practice has helped to resolve it. He concludes that, although traditional governance was highly authoritarian, post-Independence practice has been largely democratic. His overall appraisal is summed up in the title of his chapter: "A Paternalistic Democracy."

Writing in the mid-1980s, Picard (1987) focused on state structures and institutional processes in relation to what he terms the "sociocultural context." He argued that the socio-economic elite – a major part of which constituted the bureaucracy – had access to the public policy process, which it used to steer economic development. The result was expansion of mining and cattle but little else. Especially neglected was non-livestock rural production. In Picard's view, it is not democracy that has yielded this outcome; rather, it is the continuity of the BDP's unchallenged control of the state system from the early 1960s onwards.[60]

Another major contributor to the debate about the character of modern Botswana's government is K. Good, a political scientist. Pointing to the extensive constitutional powers of the president, the variety of legal instruments to control information and opinion, the lack of individual rights, and extremes of income inequality, Good (1997) characterizes Botswana's system as "authoritarian liberalism."

Pointing out that voting is necessary but not sufficient to control self-aggrandizement on the part of leaders, Good (2002) is especially critical of the BDP's elitism and non-accountability. He cites the example of the "near collapse of the National Development Bank (NDB) under the burden of unredeemed loans" (119), while many leading ministers, as well as President Masire and his brother, were in arrears to the NDB. Good's most scathing criticism, however, applies to government's "routinized injustice" towards the San people. He concludes that Botswana's democracy will remain dysfunctional as long as the poverty of the San endures. Good makes it clear that Botswana does not meet duToit's second criterion for democracy – that, in making claims against the state, citizenship be of equal value to all.

DuToit (1995) is more sanguine about the condition of Botswana's democracy, perhaps because he compares Botswana with South Africa and Zimbabwe. He argues that the numerous cultural and intra-Tswana rivalries held the potential for a divided society. Yet Botswana has built a strong state. He cites several decisions under Khama's early leadership that led to the strengthening of the state: the separation of state personnel from politics; the transfer of land allocation from the chiefs to the state; the incorporation of customary courts into the state legal system; the ongoing presence of significant expatriate personnel in the public service; and the co-optation of potential chiefly challengers, such as Linchwe of the Bakatla. An important consequence of a strong Botswana state is that its institutions have not become the personal domain of the incumbent ruling party. DuToit attributes this to a "mutual hostages" relationship between the state and the coalition of interests supporting the BDP.

DuToit recognizes that the interests of those supporting the BDP have played an important part in determining the path followed. Further, that path created gains for most Batswana, in large part because the state focused on the provision of public goods. In emphasizing these phenomena, duToit is implicitly accepting a "political economy" approach to the analysis of state power.[61] Finally, he reasons that, even though democracy and rapid economic growth have gone together, Botswana's democracy may not be sustainable. Threats to sustainability lie in: (1) the emerging shortage of grazing land; (2) the potential unravelling of the internal discipline of the BDP, which might open deep divisions along class, regional, and/or ethnic lines; and (3) the instability of the region, especially the potential collapse of the state in one or more of the neighboring countries.

In a recent book Samatar (1999) focuses on class and leadership in characterizing Botswana's governance. He contrasts "the indiscipline of the dominant class and the ineptitude of state managers" elsewhere in Africa with Botswana's "disciplined and legitimate political leadership of the dominant class." And he credits that leadership with "developing state capacity and ensuring that public power and resources are not used for personal gain" (11–12). While he acknowledges that the country's development strategy was primarily in the interests of the dominant class, Samatar finds it "astonishing that they managed to do this without pervasive rent-seeking or corruption" (177). This outcome he attributes to (1) the state apparatus being insulated from the rent-seeking tendencies of the dominant class members and (2) the leadership of Seretse Khama.[62]

In sum, the basic data show Botswana's strong economic record and an evolution of governance from traditional tribal chieftaincies to a modern democratic republic.

2

Growth and Democracy:
The Issues

Given the evolution of Botswana's political system from tribal chieftancies to an independent democratic republic, and given its strong economic performance since Independence, the obvious question arises: is there a relationship between Botswana's growth and its democracy? If so, then does the relationship move from democracy to growth or from growth to democracy? Or is it a simultaneous relationship, with each affecting the other?

To explore this nexus of issues, I first offer a brief review of the fundamentals underlying growth. Second, as economic policy choices are affected by the interaction between economic interests and the political system, I review the relationship between interests and policy choice within a democratic society. Third, I consider the evolution of Botswana's institutions and their bearing on economic and political choices.

I. GROWTH

Economic growth occurs with the production of additional real output. That additional output may be produced either by employing additional inputs or by obtaining more output from the same or fewer inputs, thereby improving technology. Over the past fifty years, various theories of economic growth have focused on different elements in this process. Neoclassical growth theory looks at the growth of primary factor inputs and at improvements in the technology used to combine those inputs so as to produce output. Generally, it does not explain why increases in inputs arise or what causes improved technology (Solow 1956, 1957).

Some theories start from a neoclassical base but focus on the constraints facing a developing country (e.g., shortages of capital, foreign exchange, or, more broadly, absorptive capacity) (Chenery and Strout 1966). Others focus on the importance of key inputs such as human capital (Schultz 1981). The "vent for surplus," or "linkages," theory, derived from the early growth experience of various primary exporting countries (such as Canada), sees growth arising when a primary export is sold on world markets for more than the marginal cost of production, thus generating a "surplus" of investable funds (Caves 1965). Linkages between the expanding activity and the rest of the economy create additional high-payoff activities in the domestic economy where the surplus could be invested, thereby enhancing the nation's endowment of productive factors.

The financial sector contributes to the process of economic growth (McKinnon 1973). It mobilizes savings, evaluates innovations, and channels additional resources towards activities that have the potential for success. Some opportunities are riskier than others, and an efficient financial sector manages that risk. Further, effective financial institutions monitor entrepreneurs, constantly reallocating finances as projects reveal their potential.

Recent literature suggests that economic growth is the result of improved technology. A major strand in this literature points to the importance of technological innovations and their diffusion. The fundamental source of innovations is the constant search for better and cheaper ways of producing goods and services, along with the increasing number of firms that learn from that search (Harberger 1998). In economies where successful searching and learning occurs, outdated and unsuccessful methods quickly fall away (Aghion and Howitt 1998).

An eclectic approach to the process of economic growth suggests a potentially virtuous circle. First of all, a search mechanism continuously identifies high-payoff activities such as new avenues for cost reductions. Second, entrepreneurs, financiers, and governments commit investable resources to those activities with high expected returns. Finally, the growth process perpetuates itself when each round of high-payoff activities spawns additional high-payoff activities, either in the same sectors or via linkages in other sectors, and investable resources are committed to take advantage of them.

However, this virtuous circle could be broken at any point. If expected returns are such that no search for high-payoff activities occurs, then growth never starts. If the initial returns are consumed so that no further investable resources are available, then growth is stopped. When no additional high-payoff activities are identified, or when the activities do not yield their opportunity cost, growth will soon halt. When constraints are placed on economic agents, making it impossible for them to respond to the incentives, or when entrepreneurs find it more profitable to invest in unproductive rather than in productive enterprises, growth will not happen. Finally, when the entrepreneurs and financiers face considerable uncertainty about the nature of the future economic climate, they will hold back on committing real resources to both actual and potential projects.

In Chapter 3, where I look at the evolution of Botswana's policies, politics, and institutions, I identify the nature and extent of the relationship between the virtuous circle of growth and interests, interacting in Botswana's institutional setting.

2. INTERESTS AND POLICY CHOICE IN A DEMOCRACY[1]

In Chapter 1 I showed how Britain concluded its protectorate over Bechuanaland in 1966, after first negotiating a new Constitution and administering democratic elections in 1965 to select the government. The Botswana Democratic Party (BDP), led by Seretse Khama, won the first election with 80% of the popular vote. Since then, the BDP has continued to garner well in excess of 50% of the popular vote in regular democratic elections. In Chapter 3 I look at the array of interests in Botswana, the working of government, and the policies pursued by the BDP government since Independence. This helps us answer such questions as: Were the voters choosing on the basis of their interests? Were those interests reflected in the policies pursued by the BDP? Does this ongoing democratic system help to explain why Botswana pursued growth-promoting policies? Before doing this, however, a discussion of the general literature on democracy will help us to interpret the Botswana experience.

This literature does not yield unambiguous answers to the questions just posed. One strand argues that, in a manner analogous to the Pareto optimum (in which it is not possible to make one person better off without making another person worse off), a democratic system tends to yield a social optimum that maximizes a nation's wealth. Donald Wittman (1989) argues that, in a modern democracy, the market for government is highly competitive. Political entrepreneurs are rewarded for efficient behaviour and, consequently, democracies produce efficient results. Wittman admits that political failure may occur; however, political failure is no more prevalent than is market failure. Models of political failure must assume that one or more key ingredients of efficient markets are absent. Wittman concludes that democratic political markets work as well as do economic markets.

Another strand of the literature attempts to determine why one would expect political failure. Most prominent among these authors was Mancur Olson. Building on his earlier work on problems of collective action, Olson (1993) argues that, because individuals respond to individual incentives, there is a tension between collective interests and specific interests. Individuals may be rational wealth maximizers, supporting those candidates who would maximize the voter's individual wealth. But that does not imply that a democratic society would collectively choose to maximize its wealth. As Drazen (2000) shows, a society may display a considerable heterogeneity of interests. If individuals with heterogeneous interests vote for politicians and policies that would maximize each voter's individual wealth, then the outcome may be considerable redistribution of wealth.[2] For Olson (1996) this offers an important explanation of differences in incomes across countries: when appropriate collective arrangements are missing there are "Big Bills Left on the Sidewalk."

Redistribution alone may not reduce wealth as it may be conducted in a non-distortionary manner. However, redistribution policies certainly can adversely affect economic performance. Adam and O'Connell (1999), for example, model the deleterious effects of redistribution – from the private sector to government – on the efficiency of investment and, hence, on growth. This may help to explain Botswana's declining total factor productivity (see Chapter 4, below).

A somewhat different explanation for suboptimal performance is modelled by Lizzeri and Perisco (2001). The choice between providing goods and services that "cannot be easily targeted to subsets of the population" (255) and (inefficient) targeted pork-barrel redistribution depends on the relative value of the two to the voters. The less valuable the non-targeted (public) goods, the more likely that the government will choose to provide pork-barrel goods targeted to a specific group. In Lizzeri and Perisco's simple model, the electoral system affects this choice. A winner-take-all system (as opposed to a proportional representation system) will switch to pork-barrelling when the value of non-targeted goods declines to the point where a simple majority of voters gains more from redistribution. The fact that Botswana's electoral system is winner-take-all may thus help to explain the changing nature of the policy mix.

Stiglitz (1988) argues that government failure is just as much a problem as is market failure. And the distribution of current income may not be all that is affected by political forces. Besley and Coate (1998) develop a model of political failure in an environment where, due to the fact that political control does not extend into the future, potential Pareto improvements do not get made.

Related to the time horizon problem, there is an extensive literature, reviewed by Drazen (2000, chap. 4), on what is known as the time-consistency problem. This problem arises because a government may initially promise one thing but then find it optimal to do something else. Investors' response to the potential for time-inconsistent behaviour on the part of governments is to minimize their exposure. This problem is particularly important for a new country and/ or a country in which much of the foreign investment, once made, is a sunk cost (e.g., it goes to infrastructure or mineral extraction). Both the time horizon problem and the time-consistency problem were key challenges facing Botswana's government in the late 1960s.

The theoretical literature is augmented by cross-country empirical studies, which consider ethnic diversity to be one dimension of heterogeneity. This has led some authors to cite ethnic diversity as a potentially important factor associated with poor economic growth performance. Mauro (1995) finds a significant relationship between "ethnolinguistic fractionalization" (defined as the probability that two randomly selected persons in a given country would not belong to the same ethnolinguistic group) and institutional inefficiency. The latter, in turn, is associated with corruption and poor economic performance.

Easterly and Levine (1997) assume that ethnically diverse countries are less likely to have effective mechanisms for mediating conflict than are ethnically homogeneous countries. For this reason, they argue, ethnolinguistic diversity helps to explain some important public policies that adversely affect growth. They go on to cite Botswana's apparent ethnolinguistic homogeneity and pro-growth policies (1218). As I noted above, Easterly and Levine's measure overstates the degree of ethnic homogeneity in Botswana at the time of Independence (this is because it classified the Tswana living outside their home territories as ethnically identical to the local Tswana). Collier (2001), however, shows that fractionalization is not normally a problem in democratic societies.

The empirical literature on democracy and growth includes Barro's (1997) cross-country growth regressions. His study of the relationship between democracy and growth found that higher living standards tend to yield greater democracy but that there was only a weak effect in the other direction. The favourable effects of democracy on growth arise through such influences as the rule of law, small government consumption, and high human capital; however, once such variables are accounted for, the influence of democracy on growth is weak.[3]

In sum, the literature does not point to an automatic connection between Botswana's ongoing democratic system and the pursuit of growth-promoting policies. On the contrary, a democratic society may choose not to act in the collective economic interest. I return to these issues in Chapter 4, when I consider the political economy of Botswana's rapid economic growth.

3. INSTITUTIONS

Over the past decade or so there has been a reconfirmation of the importance of institutions for the process of economic development.[4] But what are institutions? Perhaps the clearest definition comes from North (1990, 3): "Institutions are the rules of the game in a society." North goes on to stress that institutions are the underlying determinants of long-run economic performance. One of the central "rules of the game" emphasized by Olson (2000), among many, is secure and well defined property rights.

Alesina (1998) has shown, via cross-sectional studies, that institutional quality is important for growth. It is not simply economic institutions that affect economic performance: the idea that political institutions affect economic outcomes is developed by, among others, Przeworski (1991) and Weingast (1995). However, as Drazen (2000, 61) reminds us: "Political institutions clearly matter for outcomes, but that observation alone does not tell us *which* institutional details matter."

Quality institutions are not readily created. Davis and Trebilcock (1999) conclude that establishing quality institutions to enact, administer, and enforce laws and regulations has proven a daunting challenge for many developing countries. Ultimately, the administration of the legal system cannot be distinguished from government administration more generally. In the Botswana case, as I discuss in more detail in Chapter 3, the quality of the government administration is an important element in the evolution of the modern state.

Olson (2000) argues that a second condition, beyond secure and well defined property rights, must be met if there is to be economic progress in a market economy: the absence of predation.[5] If predation is possible, then potential predators spend real resources on offensive mechanisms to capture goods from potential prey, who, in turn, spend real resources on defensive mechanisms to protect their property. Olson reasons that a single predator who controls a given territory has an encompassing interest and, therefore, becomes a "stationary bandit," functioning as a monopolist in his predation, thereby limiting the amount of predation and the cost to society.[6] It follows that a democracy, which has an even more encompassing interest than does the stationary bandit, would seek to further limit predation.

Yet we observe regimes, from dictatorships to democracies, that tolerate predation on a scale that is clearly damaging to both their economy and their society. Given the reduction in the income of regime leadership, why would it tolerate predation? The answer offered by various contributors to the political science literature focused on weak states or, more specifically, on weak state institutions.[7] If Olson's "stationary bandit" would not find it rational to countenance predation, then why would any well defined regime choose such an outcome? We need an explanation for the underlying conditions that yield predation.

One promising line of reasoning is as follows. Consider a regime[8] consisting of a small number of individuals with identical interests. To further its interests, the regime employs a set of policies. If members' interests are identical, then the regime faces the same incentives as does the stationary bandit. But if there are heterogeneous interests, then differences between members across policy alternatives emerge. However, as long as the numbers in the regime leadership remain small, Coasian bargains are possible. However, given heterogeneity of interests, as the number of regime members grows, the problem of achieving consensus within the regime becomes more difficult. In the absence of a leader who recognizes the importance of regime solidarity, the outcome may be inferior to that of the stationary bandit. In other words, "leadership" that defines and articulates the regime's collective interest may be a "critical institutional detail."

If the regime is in some degree responsive to the society, as with a Cabinet in a democracy, then the issue of how to bolster support for the regime emerges.[9] To keep the story simple, suppose that regime support is maintained by a patronage pool that is financed by a non-distortionary head tax. Each member of the regime has access to the patronage pool. If the division of the pool is not specified (and enforced), then each member of the regime would have unlimited access to the pool, and the well known common property resource problem would emerge. If one member draws more of the common property resource, then there is less available to the rest. The problem arises because the individual has no incentive to take into account the effect of his/her actions on others. In the absence of some intra-regime allocation mechanism, each individual member of the regime would draw as much as he/she could from the pool because there is no cost to her/him. The effectiveness of the patronage pool in maintaining support for the regime is diluted because its use is unrelated to the regime's collective objectives. To avoid this outcome, the regime leadership either devises an allocation mechanism for the existing pool or expands the patronage pool.[10] If the latter choice is made, then the following question is critical: is the expansion of the patronage pool done in a more or less predatory manner? If the patronage pool is financed in an increasingly predatory manner, then the degree of predation expands and society's well-being deteriorates. It is the mediation of this conflict between the collective interest and specific interests that requires an explicit institutional mechanism. It is the absence of such an "institutional detail" that yields predation.[11]

Even if the regime's collective interests are clearly articulated, and the leadership is capable of controlling the distribution of the patronage pool, there remains a potential problem. If the day-to-day activities of government are not well administered, then the desired effect of policies will not be achieved. This is a particularly serious issue for new countries, where the functioning of government cannot be taken for granted. In other words, the effective execution of the government's intention may be a further critical "institutional detail."

Not only are institutions important but the relationship with growth is a complex matter, with many different channels of influence – from institutions to growth and from growth to institutions (Aron 2000). Empirically, Barro's (1997) work has elucidated the complex two-way relationship between the overarching political institution – democracy – and growth. Further, the choice of institutions is fundamentally a political decision and, thus, must be linked with the nation's politics. Acemoglu and Robinson (1999) recognize this as they model endogenous institutional choice. Moreover, since institutional arrangements are highly interrelated, they are not readily subject to piecemeal tampering (Rodrik 1999).

There is no unique ideal set of preferred institutional arrangements for any society, although clearly some combinations are preferable to others. With that in mind, what are the important mechanisms whereby institutions affect economic policies that might be relevant in the Botswana context? A useful starting point is to recall the fact that the outcome in any collective decision process will depend both on the preferences of the individuals involved and on the rules pertaining to collective decisions.[12] Those rules, in turn, depend on the political system and on the history of the polity.

Two recent contributions emphasize the importance of history in explaining today's institutional structure for any given country. Engerman and Sokoloff (1997) start from the initial conditions of factor endowments in the Americas to explain the evolution of economic institutions that shaped the economic growth that followed. Differences in factor endowments affected the type of economic activities carried out, which, in turn, influenced the initial income inequality. This income inequality, for its part, retarded economic growth.

Acemoglu, Johnson, and Robinson (2001) look at the effect of institutions on today's GDP per capita in former European colonies. Since institutions are in part endogenous, they need to identify some independent source of institutional difference. They find that, where Europeans could settle, European institutions were retained, establishing the basis for today's institutions. Where Europeans could not settle in their colonies because of disease, they typically set up exploitative institutions that were not growth-promoting.[13] They recognize that the colonial experience was but one of the many factors affecting institutions. Yet once they control for the effect of institutions on income per capita, the commonly cited influence of Africa and distance from the equator disappear.

Institutions are linked to interests in several ways, but perhaps most significantly by the fact that interests have a major influence on the choice of institutional arrangements. Those institutional arrangements then tend to be self-reinforcing. There are several distinct reasons for this. First, the existing policy bias gives rise to investments based on existing institutional arrangements. Those investments, in turn, enhance the interests of those dominating existing institutions.

Second, many institutions are public goods, which, by their nature, are available to all members of a society.[14] The cost of a public good is typically far greater than an individual can bear. Hence, individuals are unwilling to participate directly in the creation of a public good. Consequently, in the absence of government provision, certain institutions may be missing. Yet once government is providing a public good at no cost to the individual beneficiaries, the benefit for most exceeds the cost (at the margin). Hence, a constituency of net beneficiaries is created.

Third, technocracies may be an important part of institutional structures. Politicians may delegate policy design and implementation to technocracies, which then champion the continuation of the policy thrust. Bates (1999) notes that politicians can monitor the impact of the technocrats and their policies on the politicians' interests and, therefore, only empower those technocrats whose policies support their interests.

For all these reasons – investments, public goods, and technocracies – interests are created that tend to reinforce the existing path. This, I argue, is a significant feature of the Botswana experience.

The literature identifies two sets of institutions that have been particularly important for Botswana: agencies of restraint and institutions for conflict management. Collier (1996) identifies agencies of restraint as critical in reducing the uncertainties facing private investors. Different types of restraints are needed to bind government's macroeconomic policies,[15] to curb corruption among government's employees, and to verify information and enforce contracts between private agents.

Institutions for conflict management, as emphasized by Rodrik (1999), are important in restraining actions that might otherwise be taken. When changing circumstances change the returns to different interests (or ethnic groups) social conflict is triggered. But where there are institutions that promote social cooperation, societies are more likely to persist on good policy paths. For example, limits on gains for the winners and losses for the losers may obviate the need to resort to macroeconomic imbalance to restore political equilibrium.[16]

I turn now to a review of the evolution of major economic policies in Botswana. In doing so I focus on how certain policies affected economic growth and how they were shaped by specific interests and institutions. My account is inevitably selective, yet it should become clear that the elements upon which I focus are among the major reasons why the Botswana case is different from any other and, hence, vitally important for a full understanding of the Botswana experience.

3

Evolution of Policies, Politics, and Institutions, 1966–2000

The advent of Independence in 1966 did not halt the evolution of Botswana's politics and institutions; rather, with the Constitution having set the "rules of the game," the political contest and the institutional arrangements defining and constraining government now worked within a new framework, albeit one that was in keeping with Tswana traditions. The policy thrust and, in turn, economic growth were clearly influenced by the new environment. In this chapter I begin by looking at the baseline of interests at Independence and then turn to a review of key elements in the post-independence evolution of institutions, policies, and politics.

I. INTERESTS AT INDEPENDENCE

The BDP had captured a substantial majority of the electorate in the 1965 elections. Consequently, the party had an incentive to pursue policies that did not impose an excess burden on the economy as that burden would have been borne by the majority of society, which the BDP represented. The BDP clearly had what Mancur Olson (1982) described as an "encompassing interest" in the society. But it had more than simply an encompassing economic interest: the BDP captured the votes of the numerical majority and bridged potential tribal differences. Further, given the decision by the British to proceed with Independence, the interests of the political majority, the old and new political elite,[1] and the economic elite all largely coincided. In other words, there was a considerable degree of ex ante homogeneity of interests and, therefore, little tension between either ethnic or political interests on the one hand, and economic interests on the other.

At the time of Independence, the vast majority of the people of Botswana were rural, cultivating subsistence crops and tending cattle. While the distribution of cattle ownership was highly skewed, there was no significant alternative form of income or wealth that might have become the focus of an intersectoral political contest, and even the non-cattle-owning residents of the rural areas had an indirect interest in the health of the cattle sector. Further, since cattle and beef were the principal exports, the joint economic interest of all those involved in the cattle sector lay in maintaining Botswana's external competitiveness. It is clear, therefore, that from the beginning both the political majority and the economic elite had an interest in a competitive real exchange rate.

Similarly, the potential basis for a political contest between factors of production was limited. In cattle production, because land was effectively a free good at the margin, and because capital and labour were both mobile, there was no fixed factor that would bear the brunt of discriminatory policies. Infra-marginal land was the only potential victim of discriminatory policies. In the past it had been allocated by the chiefs, and, at the time of the 1965 election, the BDP was careful not to alienate the elite, explicitly promising that "the individual and communal rights of ownership will be respected."[2] Nevertheless, there was a clear potential for a divergence of interests based on ethnicity. Known mineral deposits were not evenly distributed across the tribal areas, and individual tribes could legitimately claim those deposits based on their land rights.

2. WORKING OF GOVERNMENT

Following Independence, the day-to-day workings of government evolved in ways that proved important for the future. Several features stand out. First, the consensus-seeking approach to government, which had deep roots in Tswana culture, dominated. For example, draft Cabinet memoranda on proposed policies were circulated for comment among all relevant ministries, and only after an inter-ministerial consensus had been attempted would a memorandum go forward to the Cabinet. This process, in turn, became institutionalized in the form of regular consultations within ministries and inter-ministerial working groups dealing with ongoing policy issues, thus reinforcing the culture of consensus.

Second, in keeping with the consensus-seeking approach, the practice of naming a "presidential commission" to investigate the options and to propose a policy framework was frequently adopted for particularly difficult or complex problems. The resultant report, usually a consensus of the commission membership, would then form the basis for a "government paper," commonly referred to as a "white paper," spelling out the proposed policy course and underlying rationale. In adopting this approach, government risked facing recommendations that it did not favour, but it proved willing to do this.

Third, many individual ministers served for extended periods in the same portfolio. For example, Masire served as vice-president and minister of finance (later finance and development planning) from the time of the internal self-government (1965) to his assumption of the presidency on the death of Khama (1980). Similarly, many senior civil servants remained in the same ministry for extended periods. In the process, both ministers and their senior advisors became highly knowledgeable about the policies and problems of their ministries, and developed institutional memories. An important side effect of knowledgeable ministers and senior civil servants was that ministerial briefings were not mere pro-forma exercises; rather, they were often occasions when policy options were presented, analyzed, and discussed.

Fourth, in assembling the modern government apparatus, Botswana drew heavily on foreign technical assistance, from the British initially, but soon from many other donors. Given the very limited stock of educated Batswana, such personnel were clearly required if the standard of public administration was to be sustained at a quality necessary for rapid growth. While these needs might be attributed to British neglect during the decades of the Protectorate, the Botswana government adopted a very pragmatic approach. President Khama made it clear that "we should never sacrifice efficiency on the altar of localisation" (Fawcus and Tilbuy 2000, 218). The political leadership was more interested in ensuring the effective functioning of the economy than in pointing blame, and it saw this goal as being best accomplished through efficient governance.

The operational style of the diverse set of technical assistance personnel contrasted with that of many of the old colonial service personnel who had relied on a hierarchical style of management. The technical assistance personnel were more interested in "getting it right" and in working with their newly trained Batswana colleagues than in observing a rigid hierarchy. They provided more than mere stop-gap staffing of ministries: many became associated with Botswana for extended periods, and some stayed and took out citizenship. Not only did they contribute to a relatively efficient government, but they also facilitated the transmission and application of ideas and technologies from around the world to Botswana. In contrast with "two-week experts" intent on applying a "one-size-fits-all" template to this fortnight's assignment, or pushing the agenda of their funding agency, many of the long-term technical assistance personnel became knowledgeable about the nuances of local circumstances, including the institutional capacity to implement agreed-upon policies.

Fifth, the development planning process, which had begun with the pre-Independence request for multi-year assistance, continued after Independence. At first this was because, for a number of years, the need for financial assistance from Britain continued. As other donors began to contribute, the National Development Plans (NDPs) proved an important plus in attracting donor money. The NDPs focused on projecting an honest picture of expected revenues and setting priorities for desired expenditures. This reflected traditional attitudes (shaped by the harsh climate) towards good times and bad times: the value of saving during times of plenty and sharing during times of drought. Particular attention was paid to the phasing in of the operating costs of new projects, including those in the projections.

Central to the success of the NDPs was the role of Masire. As minister, vice-president, and BDP secretary general, he carried considerable clout in cabinet and the governing party. Under his leadership, the planning process was not a mere public relations exercise to attract donor funds, to be ignored in actual practice; rather, it became a central part of the process of government. Each NDP would go forward to Parliament for debate and approval only after it had been debated within government and a consensus had been achieved. The final step in that process was a multi-day discussion in the Economic Committee of Cabinet, which consisted of senior civil servants and the Cabinet, and was chaired by the president. Projects that could not be accommodated within the consensus plan could not be funded and would have to wait to be reconsidered in the next round. The planning process would not have been effective without financial controls, which prevented ad hoc funding for projects outside the plan.

The NDPs articulated government's policies on a wide range of issues, not just on narrow economic questions. For example, the *NDP 1973–78* explained that the plan was formulated in the context of "Botswana's five national principles, which are rooted in Botswana's past traditions and culture. These are: "democracy, development, self reliance, unity, social harmony."[3] The latter two national principles were particularly important in light of the potential for conflict arising from the underlying ethnic diversity noted earlier. Since Independence policies have been formulated in the name of unity and social harmony and have deliberately avoided any ethnic references. In light of circumstances elsewhere in Africa, including neighbouring South Africa, this emphasis on unity and social harmony is scarcely surprising. For some, however, it could be seen as a mechanism to ensure the dominance of the Tswana language. For example, from the beginning, the language of instruction in schools throughout the country is Setswana, with English being added later. No instruction is given in minority languages, even in areas where the minority is the majority. And then there are the problems facing the minority Basarwa.[4] Rather than creating a policy to deal specifically with their needs, the government created a policy to provide services to "Remote Area Dwellers."

Finally, in the Botswana polity the judiciary developed as a competent independent force. In parallel with the use of expatriates in the civil service, the judiciary was often staffed by experienced foreign nationals who served for extended periods. On repeated occasions, the judiciary brought government up short, declaring specific government actions illegal. Unlike many other governments in the region, the Botswana government chose to accept such rulings rather than to change the legislation to circumvent the constitutional restriction on its action.

3 . MAJOR POLICIES

Why did Botswana prosper? In its simplest form, the answer is: because it followed growth-promoting policies. Not all policies were always growth-promoting; however, overall they certainly were. Among the most important policy areas were: minerals, land and agriculture, international trade, money, exchange rate, fiscal revenues, fiscal expenditure, labour market, and state-owned enterprises. I now review each of these.

Minerals

A key policy stance adopted at an early stage by Khama's BDP concerned mineral rights. Two issues required attention. First, traditional rights to land and, implicitly, the minerals underground were vested in individual tribes. If these rights were left unchanged, then a chief in whose territory a major mineral discovery happened to lie would have considerable economic and political power. In the early 1960s, most of the known mineral deposits and the major initial finds were located in the tribal territory of Khama's own Bamangwato,[5] forcing Khama to choose between his tribe and the nation. Second, in the past, some mineral rights had already been ceded to private companies in parts of the country.

Khama's choice was made clear in the BDP *Election Manifesto* for 1965:

Consequently leaving mineral rights vested in tribal authorities and private companies must necessarily result in uneven growth of the country's economy, as well as deprive the Central Government of an important source of revenue for developing the country ... [I]t will be the policy of the BDP Government to negotiate with all parties concerned the take over of the country's mineral rights by the Central Government, and subsequently expand the present mining operations and step up prospecting activities throughout the Territory. (Bechuanaland Democratic Party 1965, 6)

After Independence, the central government legislated itself as holder of mineral rights in tribal lands. It dealt with the private concessions by levying a mineral rights tax,[6] which could be reduced to zero by engaging in sufficient exploration. This policy (1) stimulated exploration where there was a genuine prospect of finding a mineral deposit and (2) led to the surrender of inactive mineral concessions to the state (Gaolathe 1997).

Khama's choice of vesting mineral rights in the central government would prove to be the key to establishing the authority of the nation-state. Rather than choosing to favour his home tribe, and thereby risk losing support else-where in the country, Khama chose to direct the state's share of the mineral wealth to national purposes. However, doing this required the discovery of valuable mineral deposits and, upon doing this, ensuring that the state would capture some of the wealth.

Several international companies had conducted an active minerals exploration program in the years leading up to Botswana's Independence in 1966. This was reinforced by a very active geological survey program, which continues to this day. Among the successful prospecting endeavours was that of the diamond company DeBeers, which discov-ered a substantial diamond deposit shortly after Indepen-dence. This was followed by the discovery of an even larger diamond deposit in the 1970s.

With the discovery of significant minerals deposits, the Botswana government faced the task of devising a minerals taxation policy. In some respects, small, poor Botswana appeared to be at a significant disadvantage in negotiations with major international mineral companies. Yet Botswana's pragmatic approach led to substantial investment on the part of international companies, which, in some cases, yielded considerable revenue for the central government.

Government recognized that the value of any deposit was subject to considerable uncertainty. In such circumstances, a fixed royalty rate could turn out to be charging far more or far less than the rent attributable to the deposit. Rather than relying solely on a high fixed royalty rate, government focused on obtaining for the nation a significant share of the profits from the mining operation. This was accom-plished by requiring, in addition to a modest royalty, that government be provided, at no charge, a portion of the equity in the mining operation.[7] This yielded government a significant share of the returns in highly profitable opera-tions (such as diamonds) and very little return on marginal operations, without damaging private investment incentives.

In addition to the question of the distribution of the return from the mineral deposits between the nation and the foreign investors, there was also the question of exercising Botswana's market power in the world market for diamonds. With a substantial share of actual, plus potential, world gem diamond production, there was clearly some market power to be exercised. Botswana bought into a strategy aimed at capturing a share of those rents by willingly cooperating with the DeBeers-led Central Selling Organization (CSO). Since Botswana grew to be a major world supplier of diamonds, and the DeBeers CSO handled the marketing of the bulk of uncut gem-quality diamonds, Botswana was able to capture considerable mineral rents.

It is clear from the foregoing that the Botswana government succeeded in getting incentives for both itself and the foreign investor pointed in the same direction – that of ensuring the profitability of the investment. Yet it is also true that Botswana had a stroke of good luck in the combination of the nature of the particular mineral and the nature of the foreign investor.

Diamond sales in any given year are subject to the vagaries of international demand, just as are the sales of many other primary commodities. However, diamonds are different. First, the fact that diamonds are storable, unlike many agricultural commodities, means that it is possible to stockpile output until the market has improved without the product deteriorating, incurring only the carrying cost of the capital tied up in the inventory. Second, the DeBeers organization was very successful in marketing the concept "a diamond is forever." This coveys not only the human lifetime commitment but also the idea that a diamond does not fluctuate in value from year to year (as do many industrial commodities). Hence, the large inventory that Botswana accumulated during the world recession in the early 1980s did not risk financial disaster through a drop in the world price. Further, the diamonds of Southern Africa are mostly found in "kimberlite pipes" (i.e., embedded in hard rock in the ground). The process of extraction occurs at a well defined location, and access to the diamonds is controlled. Hence, governments can provide a secure tenure to the mining company and monitor output for taxation purposes. This stands in contrast to alluvial diamonds, which are scattered along riverbeds. The extraction process involves individuals, or small groups, who are often in competition and lack any security of tenure over a deposit. In this situation, attempts to impose taxation often end up corrupting the tax authorities.

The Botswana-DeBeers relationship was a stroke of good fortune for both the government and the investor. In the mid-1960s, the state of Botswana was still fragile. Unlike multinationals elsewhere, DeBeers did not corrupt Botswana. This may be because DeBeers simply couldn't win at that game, or it may be because Oppenheimer was an ethical person. A major contributing factor has to be the long-term view that both Botswana and DeBeers took to the relationship. In any case, this sound relationship allowed both the state and the investor to prosper.

Not all of Botswana's mineral deposits proved to be rich and, hence, capable of generating significant revenues for government. None of the various deposits that had been exploited prior to Independence – gold, silver, kyanite, asbestos, manganese – proved to be economical for long-term exploitation in the early post-Independence years.[8] The three potential minerals mentioned in the 1966 *Transitional Plan* – copper, coal, and soda ash – have all been developed but have proved to be marginal, generating very little rent over the long term. The copper-nickel deposit at Selebi-Phikwe was developed in the 1970s but suffered major technical and economic problems.[9] Frequently, it was unable to service its debt, requiring repeated refinancing of its operations, including government forgiveness of royalties. It is now nearing exhaustion, and even with most of the capital investment either depreciated or written off, it is unlikely the mine will last many more years. The coal deposit at Morupule has been exploited to provide electricity to the national grid and, crucially, to the copper-nickel mine. However, another, much larger but lower grade, deposit has not yet been exploited. The soda ash and salt potential of the

salt pans at Makgadikgadi was finally developed in the early
1990s but had both technical problems and the bad luck of
a flood, which overflowed its evaporation facilities. It filed
for bankruptcy. Once the debt had been written off, since
much of the capital investment was sunk, it was possible
for a successor company to reopen the facility.

Despite these problems, because of unusually profitable
diamond production, mineral revenues have been sizable,
quickly becoming government's principal revenue source.
This will be seen when I review government revenues below.
The surplus thus generated was available either for investment in other parts of the economy or for predation. In
other words, the development of the mineral sector was
crucial for the subsequent stages of development but by no
means secured Botswana's future.

Land and Agriculture

At the time of Independence the mix of land tenures – traditional, state-owned, and private concessions – paralleled
that of mineral rights. However, unlike mineral rights policy, land policy directly affected virtually everybody in the
country, and there were many subtle differences in practice
across different tribes and socio-economic groups within a
given tribal district. Further, agriculture was the dominant
economic activity, and it was second only to the exploitation of mineral deposits with regard to representing the
major hope for increasing incomes.

In the tribal areas land tenure was vested in the tribe and
allocated to individuals, ultimately by the chief but in practice by a ward overseer. Every member of a tribe was entitled to the use of land for housing in the village, for crops
in the immediate vicinity of the village, and for grazing on
more distant lands. But the critical constraint for grazing
was water access. Some natural water sources existed, and
some supplementary sources were developed communally,
but the development of many water sources was the result
of private investment, which permitted the owner to

Table 3.1
Distribution of cattle wealth, 1968/69 and 1986

Size	Number of landholders		Number of cattle		Share, landholders (%)		Share, cattle (%)	
	1969	1986	1969	1986	1969	1986	1969	1986
0–10	23,810	48,700	59,712	119,200	49.9	58.5	4.8	6.1
11–50	18,136	26,400	442,240	712,800	38.0	31.7	35.8	36.5
>50	5,808	8,200	734,922	1,122,400	12.2	9.8	59.4	57.4
Total	47,754	83,300	1,236,874	1,954,400	100.0	100.0	100.0	100.0

Sources: 1968/69, National Development Plan 1970–75, 40; 1986, Botswana
Agricultural Statistics 1986, Table 18.
Notes: In 1968/69 freehold farming areas accounted for 13.6% of the national herd.
In 1986 "commercial farms" had 16.2% of the national herd. Since the commercial
farms category includes freehold farms plus commercial farms on land allocated to
citizens by the tribal land boards, the two numbers are not strictly comparable.

exclude others from access. Consequently, de facto control
over large areas of grazing land lay in private hands.

The result was a highly skewed distribution of traditional
cattle wealth, which has remained so since Independence
(see Table 3.1). Those holders of tribal lands owning from
zero up to ten cattle constituted 50% of traditional agricultural landholders in 1968/69 but held less than 5% of the
traditional cattle holdings. By 1986 that same size category
constituted nearly 60% of the traditional agricultural landholders, and its share of cattle had gone up marginally to
6.1% of traditional cattle holdings.

In addition to the highly skewed distribution of cattle
wealth, complaints about the allocation system favouring
the wealthier members of the tribes, including the royal
families, were common. Yet there was no system for appeal
of the decisions of the chief (Hitchcock 1985).[10]

A serious consequence of the land system was overgrazing.
This was partly attributable to the classic common property
resource problem: communal land with ready access to
water was overgrazed, particularly in the all too frequent
drought years. But the land allocated to individuals who
had their own private water sources also suffered from

overgrazing. The adequacy of a given area of range land for a given herd of cattle depended crucially on the year's rainfall. In some years the area would be more than enough to support the cattle, while in others, the carrying capacity turned out to be far less than necessary, although, ex ante, there was no way to distinguish which years would be good and which bad. In the bad years farmers were often too slow in reducing their herd size, and overgrazing was the result. Traditionally, the response to such overgrazing pressures had been to extend the margin of rangeland into hitherto unused land. However, with the severe drought of the early 1960s, part of the response had also been for the chiefs to favour allocation to their inner circle. Government also attempted to introduce grazing controls, but these proved ineffective.

At the same time, policy makers casting about for ways and means to increase real incomes in the country saw agriculture in general, and cattle in particular, as the principal hope. A combination of changing land tenure arrangements and opening up new grazing areas was put forward as the solution in the *Protectorate Development Plan 1963/1968* (published 1963) and was repeated in the *Transitional Plan* (1966). The BDP's 1965 election manifesto was somewhat more cautious, promising to respect individual and communal ownership of land. Yet the inequities in the system were a potentially serious problem for a democratically elected government whose power base was the rural areas. The *National Development Plan 1968–73* (1968) went further, indicating that "Government will consider the introduction of Tribal Land Boards to control the allocation of land and thereby reduce the arbitrariness of the traditional land allocation system" (Botswana 1968, 25) The balance had swung against the chiefs. Government changed the land allocation system, effective in 1970, replacing the chiefs with tribal land boards.

The land boards were generally successful in fulfilling their mandates. They relied heavily on the tribal authorities for it was they who had local knowledge of the existing allocations. However, the favouritism of which the chiefs had been accused lay in wait for the land boards. With the rapid growth of urban areas in the 1980s, land boards in the peri-urban areas faced enormous pressures to allocate preferred areas to preferred individuals. The Kweneng Land Board, whose area of responsibility included the land just to the west of Gaborone, acceded to a request from the minister of local government and lands (also the vice-president) to make an allocation favourable to the minister of agriculture (the senior minister from the district). When this became public, the resulting scandal led to the resignation of both ministers and to the appointment of a presidential commission of inquiry.[11]

The other part of the solution – opening up more grazing lands – was even less successful than were the land boards. Various projects were attempted, starting in the early 1970s, but the largest was the Tribal Grazing Lands Policy (TGLP) launched in 1975. It was intended (1) to get large-scale livestock owners to move from over-grazed communal areas into new grazing areas in the marginal sandveld and (2) to introduce modern herd management methods. This was to be accomplished by providing the ranchers with exclusive and secure tenure to the land, which they were expected to fence. Unfortunately for the project, various problems emerged (see Hitchcock 1985; Fidzani 1998). In many of the areas, it turned out that the land was not entirely unused: a significant number of residents claimed rights to the lands allocated under the TGLP. Further, there was not a large shift of cattle from previous grazing lands as the larger cattle owners preferred to keep cattle in both the old and the new areas. In the early years the rains were good, but with the prolonged drought of the early 1980s the carrying capacity of the new areas was drastically reduced, and many ranchers moved large parts of their herds back into the communal areas, exacerbating the overgrazing problem that the TGLP had been intended to overcome.

Government's promotion of agriculture as a whole was substantial. Spending on the sector grew dramatically in the

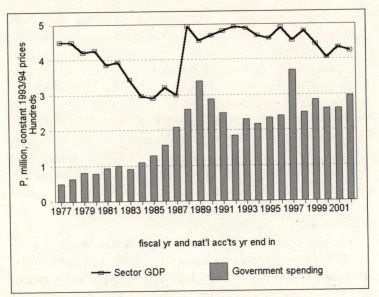

Figure 3.1
Government Expenditure on Agricultural and Sector GDP
Sources:
a. Government spending from Botswana Government, *Financial Statements, Tables and Estimates of the Consolidated and Development Fund Revenues.*
b. Sector GDP from Botswana Central Statistics Office, *National Accounts of Botswana.*

1980s, in part because of the drought that lasted from 1982 to 1987, but it has remained at an average of about half of sector GDP throughout the 1990s (Figure 3.1). Yet, as we saw in Chapter 1, real output in the agricultural sector at the end of the 1990s is no larger than it was in the mid-1970s, and it has declined dramatically as a share of GDP.

Trade

Botswana has been a member of the Southern African Customs Union from its very beginning, early in the twentieth century. Shortly after Independence, Botswana, Lesotho, and Swaziland renegotiated the long-standing customs union with South Africa.[12] The amended agreement, which came into force in 1969, yielded the smaller members an increased share of the customs union's revenue. Under the new arrangement, revenue accrued to each of the smaller members as a function of that member's own imports from *all* sources. This meant that, as Botswana's imports grew rapidly with the development of new mines and associated infrastructure (and later from rapid overall economic growth), government revenues from the customs union also grew rapidly.

While the Botswana government receives considerable revenue from the customs union arrangement, this revenue is, effectively, a tax on the consumers of Botswana as they pay protected prices on imports from all sources. Offsetting this is a price-raising effect on the modest volume of Botswana exports to customs union partners (mostly beef to South Africa), which is a transfer to the Botswana producers. The net effect of government revenue, higher prices for imports, and higher prices for exports to partners has been quantified for 1987, yielding a net cost to Botswana of about 1.25% of GDP (Leith 1992). In the years since then, the average common external tariff rate has declined, while the compensation rate has remained constant, and Botswana's net exports to the customs union have grown. Hence, it is conceivable that Botswana is now collecting a modest net return.[13]

Other effects of the customs union are also important. In the 1990s there was rapid growth of non-traditional exports from Botswana into the South African market, albeit from a small base. Botswana also has transit rights through the territory of the customs union for goods moving to other destinations. In the early years after Independence this effectively meant transit rights through South Africa and South African-controlled Southwest Africa. On occasion these rights were not honoured, but with Namibian independence in 1990, and the building of a paved road to Namibia, Botswana now has an alternative route to the sea.

As a member of the customs union, Botswana is not free to set its own import tariffs to protect domestic producers. The common external tariff is in fact the South African tariff.[14] This has meant that Botswana, unlike many developing countries, has not been free to grant nearly infinite protection to a multitude of import-substitution industries (a practice that has led to disastrous results elsewhere).[15]

Government policy also played a crucial role in securing access to markets for a key export – beef. Under the special provisions of the Lome Convention, signed in 1975, Botswana's beef exports have been able to enter the European Union market with a rebate of 90% of the EU import levy, thereby obtaining a net price very nearly equal to the internal European price. While beef exports are now modest relative to diamonds, the widespread ownership of cattle in the country has meant that the benefits of this provision have been spread over a large part of the population. It should be noted, however, that this benefit may well disappear under the new Cotonou Agreement, which replaced the Lome Convention in 2000. The current terms have been extended to the end of 2007, but under the World Trade Organization (WTO) there must be a waiver for this provision.

Monetary Policy

In 1966 Botswana's financial sector was basic. Although Botswana had been a British protectorate, the money in circulation was South African. Most of the banking services were provided by agencies that opened a few hours each week. These, and the very few permanent commercial bank branches, were branches of South African banks. At Independence Botswana chose to continue to use the South African monetary system. After a few years, with the prospect of growing revenues from minerals, Botswana decided to address the question of whether or not it should have its own currency. Together with Lesotho and Swaziland, in 1973 Botswana began negotiating with South Africa for a monetary agreement. Botswana broke off these negotiations in 1974 and began preparations for creating a central bank and its own currency. A white paper was issued in

1975, and the new currency, the pula, was launched in August 1976.[16]

This move created the need to establish policy in four areas: money, the exchange rate, exchange control, and licencing and regulation of financial institutions. These were to be followed eventually by a fifth – management of foreign exchange reserves.

Initially, the setting of monetary policy was left to the Ministry of Finance and Development Planning. The basic strategy was set out in a government white paper: to regulate interest rates "with a view to satisfying domestic business and general economic requirements."[17] As the newly formed central bank developed its ability to evaluate monetary policy options, the formulation of monetary policy evolved into a joint process between it and the ministry. For several years the idea was to change the regulated rates in response to changing circumstances. But in the first half of the 1980s circumstances began to change rapidly. Substantial balance of payments surpluses, largely due to a major new diamond mine, were not fully sterilized by offsetting increases in government balances. A significant liquidity overhang emerged.

From 1982 onwards, excess liquidity in the financial system began to grow rapidly. Although the regulated commercial bank lending rates were very low in real terms, the banks faced limited lending outlets that were not expanding nearly fast enough to absorb the growing deposits. A classic tug-of-war between the regulated and regulator ensued as commercial banks turned away deposits and frequently required depositors to hold some portion of their funds in non-interest-bearing current accounts. In the meantime, the central bank's lending rate to commercial banks was allowed to remain at roughly the rate of inflation, and its deposit rate was kept well below the rate of inflation to enable it to absorb excess liquidity.

Changes in regulated commercial bank (CB) interest rates were slow and inadequate, with the prime lending rate remaining below the rate of inflation for extended periods

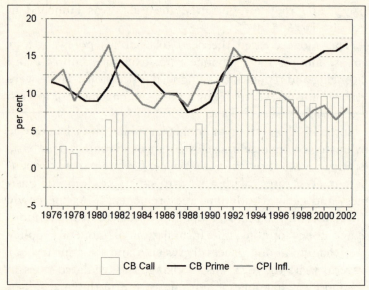

Figure 3.2
Commercial Bank Interest Rates: year end
Sources:
a. World Bank, 1989, *Botswana: Financial Policies for Diversified Growth* for 1976 to 1987.
b. Bank of Botswana, *Annual Report* for 1988 to 2002.

(see Figure 3.2). When the prime lending rate of commercial banks was deregulated in 1986, the central bank did not respond to the new situation by adjusting its own rates to absorb the build-up of excess liquidity. In the face of ongoing excess liquidity, the prime commercial bank lending rate fell below the inflation rate in 1988. Thus began a five-year period during which the CB real prime lending interest rate was negative or close to zero. With negative real interest rates, the volume of commercial bank loans accelerated dramatically (see Figure 3.3). But the excess liquidity continued to increase even more dramatically. Semi-deregulation was not achieving monetary stability.

Part of the problem lay outside the jurisdiction of the central bank. Government had long had its own window for loans to state-owned enterprises. The original purpose

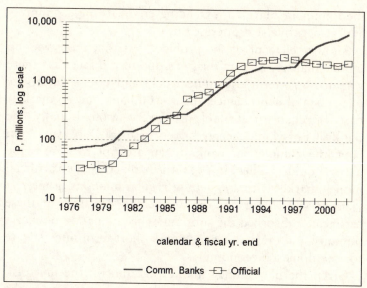

Figure 3.3
Credit Outstanding: commercial bank and official
Sources:
a. World Bank, 1989, *Botswana: Financial Policies for Diversified Growth* for
   commercial bank credit outstanding 1976 to 1984.
b. Botswana Governement, *Financial Statements, Tables and Estimates of the
   Consolidated and Development Fund Revenues,* 1981/82 and 1987/88 for official
   credit (PDSF/RSF/DF) outstanding 1975/76 to 1979/80.
c. Bank of Botswana, *Annual Report 1997* for 1985 to 1996; *Botswana Financial
   Statistics,* for all other data.

was to invest funds to ensure that government would have
adequate future funds to handle debt repayment and to
offset revenue shortfalls. The loans were made to state-
owned enterprises and local governments to finance major
capital investments. The term of the loans was set at twenty-
five years, but the rate, for the full term of the loan, was
set at a level that was normally significantly *less* than the
commercial banks' prime lending rate.

The volume of funds disbursed in this manner was substantial. By 1986 the volume of loans outstanding at the
official window exceeded the total outstanding commercial
bank loans, and it remained in that position for several
years (see Figure 3.3). In other words, government became

the dominant player in extending credit to the economy – and at negative real interest rates.

Another element of the problem was that there was no money market. In part this was due to the fact that there was no short-term government debt and very little private or parastatal debt. Hence, the central bank had no market-based mechanism available for intervention. Initially, the Bank of Botswana accepted deposits from Debswana and, later, the commercial banks in an attempt to absorb the excess liquidity. Then, in 1991, the bank created an artificial money market with a system of regular auctions of interest yielding short-term deposit certificates. The sale of these certificates absorbed the substantial accumulation of excess liquidity and created a benchmark short-term interest rate for the domestic economy.

Given the new money market instrument, the first task was to bring the interest rate on these certificates up to the rate of inflation. This was done gradually, with the interest rate catching up to the rate of inflation in early 1993. Later that year the central bank established a "target of approximate equality to real interest rates in industrial countries, with variations around this target to counter excess demand or deflationary situations."[18] By the end of 1993 the real interest rate on these certificates became significantly positive, and in 1994 it reached the indicated target, where it has more or less remained.[19]

The ultimate test of a monetary policy regime is whether or not it is able to deliver price stability to an economy. Relative to industrial countries, Botswana's record is not good. However, relative to South Africa, Botswana's former monetary partner and still principal trading partner, its record is reasonable. From the data, periods of monetary discipline and ease are remarkably clear (Figure 3.4). In the early period, the Consumer Price Index (CPI) inflation rate in Botswana followed that of South Africa fairly closely.[20] Botswana tightened both monetary and fiscal policy in 1981–82, a move associated with the diamond market downturn. The real prime interest rate was then marginally

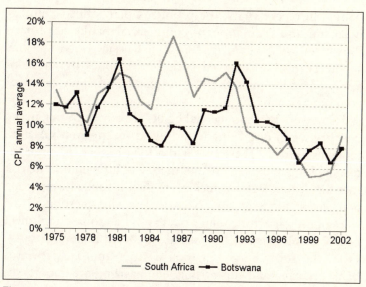

Figure 3.4
Inflation Rates: South Africa and Botswana
Source: International Monetary Fund, *International Financial Statistics.*

positive for a few years (Figure 3.2), and Botswana's inflation rate was brought below that of South Africa. It remained below South Africa for several years, in spite of the fact that the real prime rate became significantly negative. This was possible, in part, because Botswana was able to finance a substantial volume of imports to keep the excess demand from spilling over into the domestic economy and, in part, because a few of the items in the Botswana CPI basket were regulated.[21] Nevertheless, with the combination of negative real prime interest rates for the private sector, and the lending boom from government to state-owned enterprises, credit grew very rapidly in the late 1980s and early 1990s (Figure 3.3). This led to Botswana's inflation exceeding South Africa's.[22] These inflationary pressures took some time to dissipate, and it was not until 1997 that the inflation rates came together again, and then only briefly (Figure 3.4).

Beyond monetary policy, the central bank carried a second important responsibility: supervision of the commercial banks. In recent years, the problems that follow from lax licencing and regulation of commercial banks have been illustrated once again in Asia and Russia. Botswana has so far been able to avoid such catastrophes by virtue of applying strict rules for the licencing and supervision of commercial banks.

There were two commercial banks already operating in the country when Botswana withdrew from the South African monetary area.[23] These two had a long history of conservative banking in the region, and there was little immediate risk that they would become reckless in their lending, thus putting depositors' funds at risk. Nevertheless, the question of the rules of the game for commercial banks had to be established, both for the existing banks and for possible new entrants. From the start, Botswana took a strict approach towards bank licencing and supervision, emphasizing the importance of protecting depositors' interests over the interests of potential bankers and borrowers. Stringent requirements on capital adequacy and restrictions on practices such as lending to the banks own directors were put in place. Eventually, additional commercial banks were licenced.

The importance of strict banking supervision became evident on two occasions. One was when the still solvent Botswana subsidiary of Bank of Credit and Commerce International was left up in the air when the parent bank collapsed. The other occurred when another foreign-owned bank breached its capital adequacy requirements in its Botswana operations. In both cases the central bank stepped in, forcing the shareholders to arrange for an orderly sale of going concerns to another institution.

Foreign Exchange

Having created an independent currency in 1976, Botswana was faced not only with internal monetary matters but also with foreign exchange issues. These included exchange controls, the exchange rate, and management of foreign exchange reserves.[24]

Exchange controls between the Rand Monetary Area and the rest of the world were firmly in place at the time Botswana withdrew to establish its own currency. Given the uncertainties associated with the creation of a new currency, and the already existing ambience of exchange controls, Botswana chose to continue those controls. The exchange control net was applied to transactions between Botswana and the rest of the world but not to transactions between Botswana and the Rand Monetary area.

Exchange controls in Botswana have never been used to directly ration foreign exchange. Initially, almost all payment transactions were subject to exchange control formalities, but an increasing portion of these were delegated to the commercial banks. Given the very substantial foreign exchange reserves that accumulated over the years, and an exchange rate policy that focused on maintaining Botswana's competitive position (see below), exchange controls evolved into an instrument held in reserve to deal with capital account disturbances rather than with the restriction of current account payments. Gradually the restrictions were liberalized to the point were, in 1995, Botswana was accorded International Monetary Fund (IMF) Article 8 status, precluding the use of exchange controls to restrict current account payments without IMF approval. Then in 1999 the remaining capital account controls were dropped.

Exchange rate policy involved deciding on various related questions. The first was whether to adopt a fixed or a flexible exchange rate. In 1976 the South African rand was pegged to the US dollar, and many countries still used fixed exchange rates. Botswana chose to continue with a fixed exchange rate.

Having chosen a fixed exchange rate, the authorities had the ongoing task of deciding on the appropriate rate level. Over the years the currency has generally been set at a level below that which would have been indicated by a flow equilibrium. As a result, there has been a substantial accumulation of foreign exchange reserves (see Figure 1.7), amounting to about two years worth of current account payments in the late 1990s. This was a deliberate strategy employed to avoid the well known "Dutch Disease" effect, which entails a strong currency crowding out all but the most robust export activities.[25] The principal reason for this approach was that non-diamond export activities are substantially more employment intensive than is diamond mining.

In a world where all currencies are pegged, the currency to which one was pegged mattered little. However, when the rand was floated in 1979, there emerged a problem for Botswana. The pula, like most pegged currencies at the time, was pegged to the US dollar. With the rand now floating, changes in the rand/dollar exchange rate were fully echoed in the rand/pula exchange rate. This created an additional policy dimension: to which currency or currencies should Botswana choose to peg?

As noted earlier, South Africa is the major source of Botswana's imports and inward direct investment as well as the destination for most non-traditional exports. Hence both the stability and competitive position of the pula vis-à-vis the rand are of overriding importance. In the years after the rand was floated, it started to slide against the US dollar (Figure 3.5). This caused a rise in the rand/pula exchange rate, putting potential Botswana producers at a competitive disadvantage via-à-vis South Africa.

Movement of the rand/dollar exchange rate posed a serious dilemma for Botswana. The authorities could choose to have the pula follow the US dollar, the South African rand, or some combination of the two. But, given the movement of the rand/dollar exchange rate, it was not possible for the pula to remain stable against *both* the rand and the dollar. Botswana had to choose. It is clear from Figure 3.5 that, on balance, the choice was to focus mostly on the rand. In various stages the pula peg was changed from the original peg against the US dollar to a peg against a basket of regional currencies and the IMF's special drawing right (SDR), with a relatively heavy weight on the rand.

The competitive position of Botswana vis-à-vis rand- or US-dollar-based producers is not revealed by the nominal

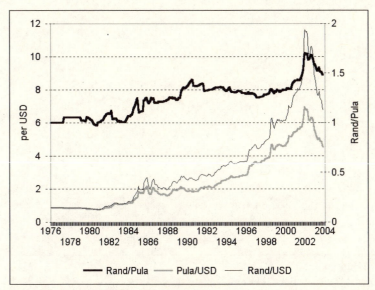

Figure 3.5
Nominal Exchange Rates: monthly averages
Source: International Monetary Fund, *International Financial Statistics.*

exchange rates in Figure 3.5. For that, one needs to look
at the real exchange rate indices in Figure 3.6. In the early
period, with a fixed exchange rate against the US dollar but
with close trade links to South Africa and its higher inflation
rate, the pula appreciated dramatically against the dollar in
real terms. Then, in the 1980s, as anti-apartheid sanctions
were introduced, the fall of the rand against the dollar,
which was only partially matched in nominal terms by the
dollar/pula exchange rate, meant that the pula depreciated
in real terms against the dollar and appreciated in real terms
against the rand. This forced the authorities to address the
question of the real exchange rate of the pula against the
rand. In the years from the mid-1980s to the mid-1990s, it
is clear from Figure 3.6 that the policy choice was to place
a heavier weight on the real competitive position of the pula
against the rand than on the pula against the US dollar. On
occasions such as those in 1988 and 1996, this meant that
the rapid depreciation of the rand created a competitive

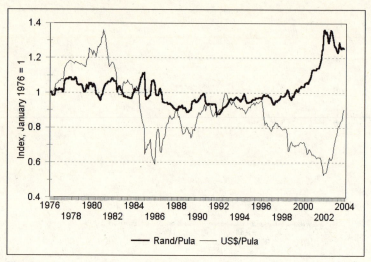

Figure 3.6
Real Exchange Rates: indexes, January 1976 = 1
Source: calculated from International Monetary Fund, *International Financial Statistics.* Note: Exchange rates refer to month end. Deflators refer to CPI of corresponding month.

windfall for Botswana vis-à-vis US-dollar-based producers and a capital loss for US-dollar-based foreign investors in Botswana.[26] From the late 1990s, however, it is evident that less weight has been placed on the competitive position vis-à-vis rand-based producers as the real rand/pula exchange rate has appreciated.

A further task fell to the central bank: management of the foreign exchange reserves. This became increasingly important as the size of the reserves grew. The function evolved from one of managing cash flow and ensuring that adequate foreign exchange was available to meet the various demands to one of handling substantial investment assets worth more than two times annual current account payments. With the cooperation of the World Bank, a strategy for investing the reserves was devised in 1988 (World Bank 1989). Commercial fund managers were engaged and were assigned performance benchmarks based on international indices, against which they were judged. At the same time, as the expertise in fund management developed within the central bank, a larger volume of the reserves was assigned to internal management.[27]

Fiscal Revenues

At Independence the Botswana government had to rely on ongoing grants from Britain to cover its regular operating budget. Much was made of the achievement in the 1972/73 fiscal year when the operating budget generated a surplus without the assistance of Britain's direct budgetary support. Nevertheless, after the phase-out of British budgetary support, for several years a significant portion of government's capital expenditure continued to be financed by foreign aid grants from various international donor agencies (Figures 3.7 and 3.8).

A well articulated and managed development planning process made Botswana an attractive destination for many international donor agencies, both bilateral and multilateral. Eventually, as its economy grew, Botswana became ineligible for many donor agency grants, and this source of revenue declined in both relative and absolute terms.

After the transition to fiscal independence, three major revenue sources dominated, as may be seen in Figure 3.8. First and foremost, the rapid minerals development generated considerable government revenue. This was augmented in important ways. The renegotiated customs union arrangement generated government revenue on imports from all sources, both from inside and outside the customs union. This meant that the import surge from mining and infrastructure development brought additional revenues to government. With the coming on stream of the second major diamond mine in the 1980s, there emerged a substantial surplus in the balance of payments on current account.[28] This was not offset by a capital outflow, resulting in a rapid accumulation of foreign exchange reserves (Figure 1.7). Earnings on those reserves became a further revenue source (classified as "property income" in government's accounts).

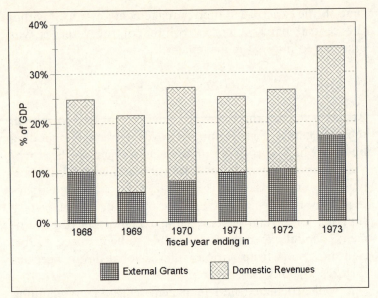

Figure 3.7
Government Revenues: 1967/68 – 1972/73
Sources:
a. Botswana Government, *National Development Plan 1973–78* for revenue data.
b. International Monetary Fund, *International Financial Statistics* for GDP series.
Notes:
a. Government fiscal year runs April through March.
b. National account years runs July through June.

Indeed, on some occasions, such as the 1993/94 fiscal year, the earnings on the foreign exchange reserves became the second largest source of government revenues.

Overall then, these three revenue sources – customs union, minerals, and foreign exchange reserves – provided 85% of budgeted government revenues in the late 1990s. It is also noteworthy that none of these appeared to fall directly on the voters,[29] and all were denominated in foreign exchange.

Total government revenues were large relative to the economy as a whole. From the early 1980s on, in most years total government revenue amounted to over 40% of GDP, and for some years even more than 50% of GDP. This situation permitted government to reduce the rates on other taxes while still keeping them in place should any one of

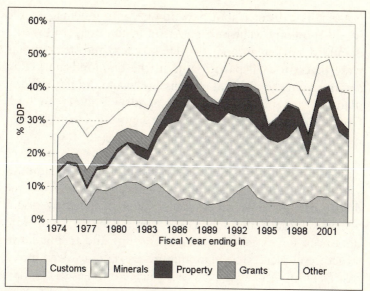

Figure 3.8
Government Revenues: 1973/74 – 2002/03
Sources:
a. Botswana Government, *Financial Statements, Tables and Estimates of the Consolidated and Development Fund Revenues.*
b. International Monetary Fund, *International Financial Statistics* for GDP series.
Notes:
a. Government fiscal year runs April through March.
b. National account years runs July through June.

the big three sources dry up. Company tax and the top marginal rate on personal income now stand at 25% of taxable income.[30]

Fiscal Expenditures

Given its revenue situation, Botswana's democratic government was faced with enormous demands to spend. Caving in to those demands could readily have put pressure on the capacity of the economy and turned rapid growth into an inflationary spiral. Those demands were countered by two important influences. First, the experience in the early 1980s of a major export shortfall made both officials and politicians cautious about spending commitments. As the world economy went into recession in the early 1980s, the diamond market suffered a severe setback, and strict quotas were placed on all participants in the diamond marketing arrangement. For several months Botswana did not sell any diamonds at all, and this had an adverse effect on both Government mineral revenues (see Figure 3.8) and foreign exchange reserves (see Figure 1.7).

Second, Botswana's system of multi-year planning of expenditures, noted earlier, served to keep total expenditures within bounds. This institution was a carry-over from the days when the bulk of the budget was financed by donor agencies. Initially, the emphasis was on raising the funds from donors to cover government's operations and to put infrastructure in place. The planning process later evolved into a relatively sophisticated exercise, which continues to this day. Desired expenditures over the projected plan period,[31] both recurrent and capital, are developed in the spending ministries and state-owned enterprises. Major policy issues facing each are articulated and resolved in the planning documents. Feasible paths of expenditure are projected by the Ministry of Finance and Development Planning. An important element in those projections is the sustainability of recurrent expenditures. Even if the capital budget is affordable in the plan period, it is trimmed if the ongoing costs cannot be covered with confidence. Priorities are then set in an extensive consultative process, which includes a series of lengthy meetings of all ministers and senior officials, and culminates in adoption of the plan by Parliament. This is supplemented by annual reviews of projects under way and an extensive mid-plan review of the overall picture.

While government was successful in implementing a macroeconomic planning process, it was somewhat less successful with regard to three important dimensions of expenditure policy: (1) consistently maintaining overall macroeconomic balance, (2) achieving the optimal share of government expenditure in the economy, and (3) maintaining an appropriate balance in the composition of government expenditure.

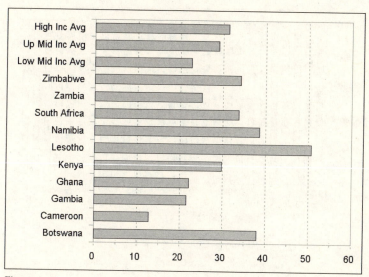

Figure 3.9
Central Government Expenditure Comparisons: percentage of GDP, 1995
Source: World Bank, World Development Indicators 2000.

Key indicators of problems encountered in maintaining macroeconomic balance have already been noted. The difficulty that government had in keeping actual expenditure and net lending on a steady growth path was shown in Figure 1.6. In part, this was a shortcoming of a planning system that had very little control over the timing of project expenditures. Another indicator of trouble in the late 1980s was the very rapid growth of official government lending (Figure 3.3). The fact that Botswana's inflation exceeded that of South Africa's in the 1990s is illustrative of these problems (Figure 3.4).

With ample funds in the bank, and in the absence of specific restraining influences, it was all too easy for government to give in to demands for particular expenditures of one kind or another. Gradually the ratio of government expenditure to GDP grew, becoming one of the highest in Africa – higher even than those of countries that have garnered a reputation for indiscipline, such as Zambia and Zimbabwe[32] (Figure 3.9). Indeed, Botswana's ratio of central government expenditure to GDP is comparable to that

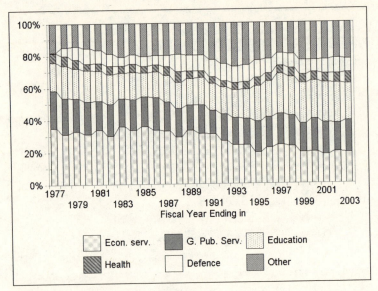

Figure 3.10
Composition of Government Expenditure
Source: Botswana Government, *Financial Statements, Tables and Estimates of the Consolidated and Development Fund Revenues.*

of Norway, and it is substantially in excess of the average of high-income countries.

Finally, it is important to observe the changing composition of government expenditure. The functional breakdown of government expenditure does not extend back into the early 1970s; however, from the fiscal year 1976/77 onwards the data are available, as is seen in Figure 3.10.

A large portion of government expenditure was spent on "economic services," consisting mostly of basic infrastructure, including electricity, water, and roads. Some of these were clearly growth-promoting as well, for without such infrastructure very little modern-sector development would have taken place. In addition, this category also includes government services to the mining and agricultural sectors. These too were growth-promoting as Botswana's comparative advantage lies in both the mineral sector and the cattle sector. The category "general public services," including government transport, buildings, police, and the courts,

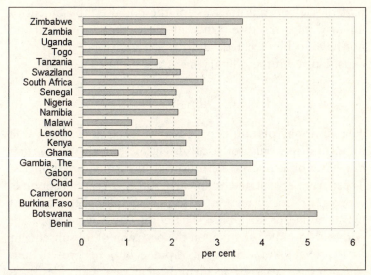

Figure 3.11
Military Expenditure, Africa: percentage of GDP, average 1991–97
Source: World Bank, *World Development Indicators 2000.*

certainly contained some waste but did not take on an ever-expanding share of government expenditure as so often happened elsewhere. Significantly for the overall growth of the economy, education expenditure grew dramatically. Health spending, while not nearly as large as education spending, was focused on the provision of primary health care throughout the country rather than on tertiary care for the urban elite.[33]

The magnitude of the military expenditure is also notable. In the 1970s Botswana was ill equipped to stand up to the hostile regimes that surrounded it in South Africa, South African controlled Southwest Africa (Namibia), and the Unilateral Declaration of Independence (UDI) regime in Rhodesia. This led to the establishment of the Botswana Defence Force. In the 1980s, as the confrontation with South Africa became more serious, Botswana suffered several cross-border incursions, and its investment in its military escalated. The result was that, in the first half of the 1990s, Botswana's military expenditure, as a proportion of GDP, became one of the highest reported in Africa (Figure 3.11).[34] A substantial part of the expenditure was for the initial establishment of military infrastructure. Once in place, that investment did not have to be repeated, and the share of total government expenditure on the military has since declined.

Labour Market

The national planning process, referred to earlier, was important not only for fiscal discipline but also for setting out basic objectives to be followed in formulating policies. These were articulated at an early stage: (1) rapid economic growth, (2) social justice, (3) economic independence, and (4) sustained production.[35] These objectives were repeated, with only a minor change, on the occasion of all subsequent NDPs. The juxtaposition of rapid economic growth and social justice was not accidental for it reflected a desire to balance the two objectives. This desire was reflected in government's approach to the labour market.

Details concerning labour market policies were set out in a government paper in 1972.[36] Two major problems were evident. There was an excess supply of unskilled workers, especially in the traditional sector, and this threatened the achievement of social justice. Simultaneously, there were serious shortages of skilled labour for the modern sector. Those shortages could trigger a bidding war among government, the state-owned enterprises, and the private sector, thereby threatening rapid economic growth.

The government followed a dual approach. In an attempt to achieve fairness, a minimum wage was established for unskilled workers. To avoid the job destruction caused by excessive minimum wages observed elsewhere, the level was to be set at "equal the average rural income of farmers with an allowance for any differential in the overall costs of urban living."[37]

When it came to policy for wages and salaries in the rest of the modern sector, government's concern with the potential for a bidding war led to a policy position whereby "wage and salary levels in the private and parastatal sectors

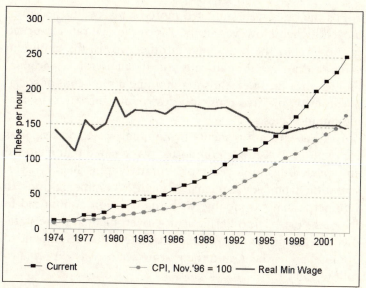

Figure 3.12
Minimum Wages: average
Sources:

a. Scoville, J. and T. Nyamadzabo, 1988, for minimum wages 1974 to 1979.

b. Botswana Central Statistics Office, *Statistical Bulletin*, December 1987 for minimum wages 1980 to 1987.

c. Bank of Botswana, *Annual Report 1997*, for minimum wages 1988 to 1997.

d. Botswana Central Statistics Office, *Labour Statistics*, for minimum wages 1998 to 2003.

e. Bank of Botswana, *Annual Report 1997*, for CPI June of each year 1974 to 1997; and *Botswana Financial Statistics*, June of each year 1998 to 2003.

should generally conform to, and on no account significantly exceed, those paid by Government to comparable grades of public employees."[38] Government would review its wages and salaries regularly and make adjustments on the basis of general economic conditions, increases in the cost of living, and increases in labour productivity.

Minimum wages were set starting in 1974. Different minima were set for different sectors, initially based on the linkage with the rural sector.[39] Taking a simple average of those rates, the pattern over time may be seen in Figure 3.12. In the 1970s the nominal minimum wages were adjusted every few years, more or less in line with inflation. In the

1980s the rates were adjusted more regularly, but real rates moved higher. However, in the 1990s the real rates returned to those set at the beginning. In other words, the minimum wage did not get dramatically out of line with the original link to rural incomes, thus maintaining a modicum of social harmony while avoiding job-destroying increases in real minimum wages.

To deal with adjustments to nominal wages and salaries for the formal sector, a committee was created that included employer and employee representatives plus heavy representation from government. It made recommendations to Cabinet, usually annually, with the decision announced in the budget speech to Parliament. Government and the state-owned enterprises were obliged to follow the recommended nominal adjustment, and the private sector was expected to follow suit.

Government's concern that the private sector would bid labour away from it proved unfounded. During the late 1980s and early 1990s, in fact, the government sector generally outbid the private sector for workers.[40] This was particularly notable in one of the key sectors of potential non-traditional employment growth – manufacturing. As is evident in Figure 3.13, government's salaries and wages grew rapidly, depressing the ratio of average monthly earnings in manufacturing relative to government.[41] The government was outbidding the private sector for available labour.

The effect of the more rapid growth of government sector wages on the balance between private- and public-sector employment was initially masked by the fact that a large part of the employment boom from 1988 to 1991 was in the construction sector, much of it financed by government, but which was almost entirely private-sector activity. As that levelled off and then declined in the 1990s, the effect became clear. Government and parastatal employment (excluding the military)[42] grew much faster than the private sector, dropping the latter's share of formal-sector employment from a peak of 65% in 1991 to 54% in 2000 before private-sector employment resumed growth (Figure 3.14).

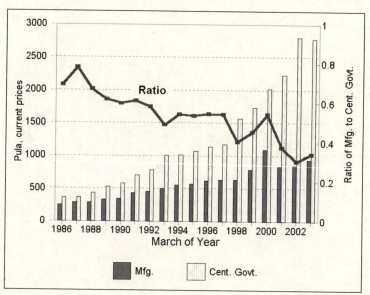

Figure 3.13
Average Monthly Earnings of Citizens: manufacturing and central government
Sources:
a. Bank of Botswana, *Annual Report 1997*, for 1986 to 1997, and *Annual Report 2000* for 1998 and 1999.
b. Botswana Central Statistics Office, *Labour Statistics.* for subsequent years.

The crowding out of private formal-sector employment via the more rapid growth of government wages and salaries stands in contrast to the crowding out mechanisms typically found elsewhere: exchange rate overvaluation and high real interest rates. On the whole, these were avoided in Botswana.

In pointing to government employment crowding out private-sector employment, I do not mean to suggest that all of the growth of government expenditure was inappropriate. On the contrary, much of it was growth-promoting, particularly the initial heavy expenditure on infrastructure, education, and health. Nevertheless, the aggregate consequences effectively offset part of the growth-promoting influences.

With the economy growing very rapidly, the shortages of skilled labour continued. The policy response to these

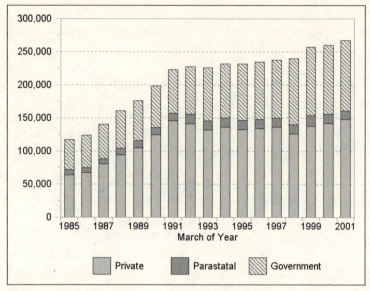

Figure 3.14
Employment in Formal Sector
Sources:
a. Bank of Botswana, *Annual Reports*, for 1985 to 2000.
b. Botswana Central Statistics Office, *Labour Statistics*, for subsequent years.

shortages was largely in the form of heavy investment in training by the public-sector, including state-owned enterprises. The remaining shortages were met by employing expatriates on term contracts. Lack of available skilled labour thus did not become an absolute constraint on the overall growth of the economy but, rather, added a cost in terms of significantly higher wage bills. The shortages were exacerbated by the fact that there were no signals from the labour market concerning what skills commanded a premium. Thus, incentives to acquire the skills to meet the shortages were absent.[43]

In the 1990s the phenomenon of youth unemployment began to emerge. The ranks of junior and senior secondary school leavers were growing much faster than was demand for their labour. Unemployment stood at 41% for the fifteen to twenty-four age group, compared to the total unemployment rate of 21% reported for the labour force as a whole in 1993/94.[44] At the same time, the structure of wages and salaries remained heavily influenced by the public service and was constrained by the "fairness" requirement. This segment of the labour market proved very slow to adjust to the rapidly changing circumstances. More generally, for those not at the leading edge of improving skills, there was typically greater supply than demand for labour.

State-Owned Enterprises

At Independence Botswana's modern sector was virtually non-existent. There was no electricity system, no telephone system, no pipe-borne water or sewage. The housing stock consisted almost entirely of the traditional rondavels. There was one five-kilometre stretch of paved road, and no nation-wide public transportation service. All the facilities for a modern economy had to be constructed from scratch.

In keeping with the approach taken in many countries, Botswana chose to rely on the state to provide essential services for the modern sector. State-owned enterprises, or "parastatals" as they are known in Botswana, were created for some functions, and other activities were simply carried out by government departments and, later, launched as state-owned enterprises (SOES).

Unlike many countries, the number of SOES and the size of the sector did not grow excessively in Botswana. Comparable data on the size of the SOE sector for African countries are limited, but the available data for the early 1990s show that Botswana's SOE sector was not exceptionally large, accounting for about 6% of GDP (Figure 3.15). This is about half the share of GDP found in neighbouring Zimbabwe. Tanzania and Zambia, notwithstanding their shared British background, have substantially larger SOE-sector shares than does Botswana.[45] Only Ghana has a similar share, but this was after many years of scaling back the SOE sector under a structural adjustment program.

Employment in Botswana's SOE sector has not ballooned. As is evident in Figure 3.14, the parastatals' share of

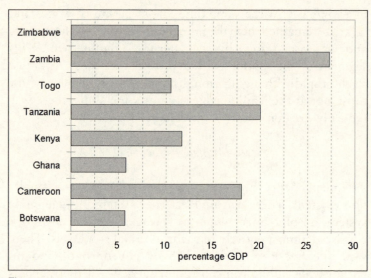

Figure 3.15
State Owned Enterprises: early 1990s
Source: World Bank, *World Development Indicators 2000.*

modern-sector employment has fallen marginally since the latter half of the 1980s.[46]

At Independence, the fundamental rationale for creating SOEs was the absence of an existing private sector in the modern economy and the urgency of putting essential facilities in place. Without water, housing, electricity, post and telephones, and transportation, nothing else could be expected to develop. As the early planning literature emphasized, each individual investor had to be able to count on the presence of a whole set of services for his/her investment to be successful. For the traditional public utilities – electricity, telephones, water and sewage, and postal services – a complementary case for government intervention certainly existed: "natural monopoly," arising from a downward-sloping average cost curve over the relevant range of demand.

The case for state involvement in other areas often involved dissatisfaction with the service provided by foreign-owned enterprises, which was perceived as retarding development. This led to the establishment of an airline and the takeover of the rail line. A similar rationale applied in the agricultural sector, where the state effectively took over the abattoir and established an agricultural marketing board to purchase grains as well as a livestock feedlot operation.

Dissatisfaction with foreign-owned financial institutions also led to the creation of several SOEs. The National Development Bank (NDB) was created in 1965 to provide loans to those neglected by the commercial banks, especially agriculture. In addition, the Botswana Development Corporation (BDC), a venture capital company capable of taking equity positions in new ventures, was established in 1970 and became by far the largest state-owned financial institution. In addition, the state initiated the Co-operative Bank, to provide financing for various cooperative enterprises; Postal Savings; and the Botswana Building Society, which took over the local operation of a South African building society.

In the area of housing, following from the state's provision of nearly all housing in the new capital, Gaborone, government chose to set up a state-owned enterprise to construct and rent out modern-sector housing. While there was no normative reason for establishing such a public-sector entity, it was in keeping with the traditional idea that land belongs to the tribe rather than to individuals.

Each of these enterprises has evolved in its own way. In the early years, the lumpy nature and substantial size of investments required for electricity, telephone, and water meant a heavy reliance on capital loans from external agencies, particularly the World Bank. Attached to each of the World Bank loans was a covenant requiring pricing to achieve a specified real return on revalued assets. This effectively prevented SOEs from becoming a drain on the public purse. The covenants with the World Bank did not, however, guarantee that all public utilities were effectively managed. The telephone company had chronic shortages of lines for new customers in the 1980s and 1990s. The postal service, which was not financed by World Bank loans, was incapable of keeping pace with the demand for new post office boxes.

State-owned institutions became significant players in the financial sector. At the end of March 1997 their total outstanding loans and investments amounted to about 5.5% of GDP, compared with the commercial banks' loans and advances of 9.3% of GDP. To this, one might add government's own loan window to SOEs. Although not a formal institution, total loans outstanding from this source stood at an additional 11.4% of GDP.[47] In other words, government itself had become a larger lender than the commercial banks and, when combined with state-owned financial institutions, became almost twice as big a lender as the commercial banks. However, since 1997 there has been a significant expansion of commercial bank lending. For example, at the end of 2000 commercial bank lending amounted to nearly 20% of GDP, while the state-owned financial institution outstanding loans had dropped back to about 4.5%, and government's own loan window had fallen in relative terms to 6.6% of GDP.[48]

The initiatives in the financial sector were undoubtedly critical in the early stages of development. The only other financial institutions were the commercial banks. The state-owned institutions were willing to invest in different projects, and for longer terms, than were the traditionally conservative commercial banks. The latter have a predisposition to protect depositors' and shareholders' interests rather than the interests of project proponents.

Managers of the state-owned financial institutions saw their primary duty as channelling loan funds into their target constituency. Needless to say, such a strategy was politically popular among those who might otherwise not have obtained loans due to, say, the risky nature of their enterprises. When arrears inevitably began to mount, and defaults became serious, state-owned financial institutions found it much more difficult to take appropriate remedial action than did private financial institutions. The performance of some of the state-owned institutions became so bad that government was forced to intervene. The NDB had to be bailed out, restructured, and subjected to external management, while the Co-operative Bank had to be closed.

The performance of the housing corporation, in contrast to that of the traditional public utilities, became a serious problem. It failed to meet the growing demand for urban housing, frequently ran substantial deficits in spite of low-interest government loans, and, in the early 1990s, was at the centre of one of the few cases of serious public-sector corruption. Numerous reports and special commissions examined the problems facing the housing corporation. The problems identified were many, and rational recommendations were made to solve them. But the central problem was that decisions to adjust rental rates were made by Cabinet. Inevitably, in the absence of any agent of restraint, Cabinet failed to keep rental rates in line with costs.

The role of the SOEs in Botswana's growth is thus mixed. Without the key part they played in ensuring the availability of essential services in the first decade or two of Independence, very little subsequent growth would have been possible. Further, they did not become a massive drain on the state, as happened all too often elsewhere in Africa. Yet, with the maturation of the economy, they became less and less necessary. But institutions, once created, tend to take on a life of their own, to develop constituencies of their own, and, thus, to persist even after they have evolved from being growth-promoting into being growth-retarding.

Industrialization

From the beginning, the NDPs cited the importance of industrialization.[49] Initially, the fundamental rationale for industrialization was diversification beyond agriculture, and then beyond minerals and agriculture. Two other phenomena – citizen economic empowerment and private enterprise – shaped the outcome.

Various initiatives were taken early on. As noted above, the NDB (1965) and the BDC (1970) were created to channel funds to areas where commercial banks were reluctant to venture. The post-Independence renegotiated SACU agreement of 1968 included clauses that permitted Botswana, Lesotho, and Swaziland to grant time-limited protection to infant industries in their own territories. It also provided for SACU as a whole to grant protection to industries in these countries capable of supplying a substantial portion of the whole SACU market. A local preference margin for government's own purchases was introduced in 1976.

The distortion arising from these initiatives was limited in the early years. The NDB was constrained by its small capital base until about 1980. The BDC typically took minority positions in joint ventures and did not attempt to become the principal source of modern-sector employment growth.[50] The SACU infant industry protection clause was invoked sparingly, initially to establish a brewery and later to establish a soap factory. Both were also granted exclusive licences to manufacture their products in Botswana. Despite, or perhaps because of, their monopoly positions, both protected manufacturers experienced serious problems in satisfying the quality and taste demands of the Botswana market, and the original investors sold out. These bad experiences effectively precluded consideration of other cases of infant industry protection.

In the 1980s further incentive programs were introduced. The overall approach was summed up in a 1984 white paper, which reflected a careful balancing of national interests in efficiency and the pressure for incentive programs.[51] For example, the policy noted: "If several incentives are given to the same project, it might result in a situation where the benefits to Botswana are less than the cost of the assistance or grants … [Therefore], Government in principle will not allow the same firm to be supported by more than one scheme at any time."[52]

The most prominent incentive program was the Financial Assistance Policy (FAP),[53] begun in 1982. FAP was intended to promote new or expanded employment-intensive non-traditional businesses. It made grants for limited periods according to various criteria but based primarily on the promise of expanded employment. Another program was the Selebi-Phikwe Regional Development Project (SPRDP), established in the late 1980s. It was specifically for the region surrounding the copper-nickel mine at Selebi-Phikwe, as the latter was experiencing serious difficulties with the combination of declining world prices and expected exhaustion of the orebody (Cowan 1997). Two fundamental problems afflicted both programs: (1) grants were made on the basis of *promises* of employment expansion but without adequate monitoring of performance, and (2) the incentives attracted footloose companies that, as the Botswana incentives phased down, would close and move on to the next location offering incentives, not infrequently leaving workers and suppliers unpaid.

Further wrinkles to the incentives were added in the 1990s with a revised Industrial Development Policy (1996), the replacement of a local preference margin by a local procurement program to explicitly channel a portion of government's purchases to small and medium local companies (1997), and the establishment of schemes to provide loans to micro-enterprises and credit guarantees for small and medium enterprises (1998).

All of these schemes were subject to increasing abuse, ranging from simply over-optimistic projections of expected employment to fronting for foreigners and outright fraud. Increasingly, government itself recognized that these arrangements were becoming a problem. In his 2001 budget speech, the minister of finance and development planning noted: "The fourth evaluation of the Financial Assistance Policy (FAP) was completed last year. The evaluation revealed, among other things, a high failure rate among small-scale FAP-assisted businesses, as well as widespread abuse of the scheme by some beneficiaries."[54] The president, for his part, "condemned the widespread abuse of government assistance schemes, describing it as wasteful of public resources which deprives other Batswana of opportunities to benefit."[55]

The SPRDP was effectively absorbed by FAP in the mid-1990s. In turn, the FAP window was closed in 2001 and replaced by the Citizens Entrepreneurial Development Agency, whose declared intention was to be much more closely involved in monitoring projects. The new agency continues, nevertheless, to offer cheap credit to marginal enterprises.

The NDB had launched an ambitious expansion program in 1980, doubling its loan portfolio in that year, doubling it again in 1981, and once again by the end of 1983.[56] In spite of government's major bail-out of agricultural debt to all banks following the drought from 1982 to 1987, the NDB became effectively insolvent in 1992.[57] A major restructuring of the NDB was then initiated, including a thorough management shake-up, and by fiscal year ending 1998 it was paying dividends to Government.

The BDC, for its part, frequently became both a lender to and co-investor with foreign direct investors, enabling the foreign investor to minimize its exposure, with the BDC shouldering most of the risk. The result was that, during the 1990s, the BDC's profits averaged a nominal 2.1% of equity,[58] substantially below the rate of inflation during the same decade. Finally, in 2000, following significant losses (including the collapse of the Hyundai motor vehicle kit assembly operation[59] in which the BDC had invested heavily), a major restructuring was undertaken.[60]

The direct outcome of these initiatives is hard to judge. Looking at the manufacturing sector, the Botswana economy is not substantially more diversified than it was at Independence, with that sector persisting at around 5% of GDP. Nevertheless, as was seen in Chapter 1 (Figure 1.2), the non-mineral non-government sector of the economy has grown in relative terms. Significantly, by consistently emphasizing the private sector, Botswana has been able to avoid the costly excesses of a bloated state-owned enterprise sector. Yet some of the failures have been costly. And some of the incentives created by a panoply of initiatives have reduced productivity and thereby slowed overall growth. I return to this issue in Chapter 4.

Starting from a baseline sketch of interests at the time of Independence, I have reviewed the evolution of Botswana's major government institutions and the policies that had a bearing on the country's economy. It now remains to interpret the evidence.

4

Interpreting the Evidence

We know that Botswana's growth record of more than three decades is exceptional. A number of countries have achieved rapid economic growth for a decade or two, but few have been able to sustain it for as long as Botswana. What is even more exceptional is the fact that the initiating source of its growth was mineral wealth, and we know that still fewer countries have been able to transform mineral wealth into sustained economic growth.

Botswana's growth was accompanied by the transformation of a fledgling postcolonial polity into an ongoing democracy. Again, this is exceptional, particularly in Africa, where few of the postcolonial democratic constitutions lasted more than a decade before being thrust aside, either by the ruling party or by the military.

Botswana's record of growth and democracy thus stands in contrast to that of the rest of Africa. But what brought this about? The previous chapter set out the evolution of Botswana's interests, institutions, and policies. It now remains to interpret that evolution. Understanding the economics is the first step in the process, but it is not sufficient, for we must also understand why the interests and institutions – in short, the political economy – resulted in growth-promoting economics. I begin with the economics and then turn to the political economy.

1. INTERPRETING THE EVIDENCE: THE ECONOMICS

Botswana's economic record has several features that make it noteworthy. First, investment rates in both physical and human capital have been high. Second, like many other developing countries, Botswana has been hit by serious shocks in the form of substantial year-to-year output fluctuations in major sectors, particularly agriculture and mining, and international terms of trade instability. Third, macroeconomic stability has been generally good, with no bouts of serious inflation and no prolonged recessions, both of which have characterized the macroeconomic history of many developing countries.

There is a remarkable consensus in the economics literature that high investment rates and macroeconomic stability are necessary if a country is to achieve sustained growth.[1] It is tempting to conclude, therefore, that Botswana's skilful macroeconomic management in achieving high investment and macroeconomic stability is the foundation upon which its growth story has been built. The implication is that a continuation of past practice will achieve similar future performances.

My interpretation of the record is more complex and subtle than this. First, while there is little doubt that macroeconomic stability was necessary for Botswana's rapid growth, in the face of major disturbances that stability was achieved by a *combination* of policies, institutions, and built-in shock absorbers rather than simply by skilful macroeconomic management. Second, given its macroeconomic stability, Botswana's rapid growth was based on high investment rates in both physical and human capital, a substantial portion of which was either directly or indirectly government's investment. Initially, those investments in infrastructure and education had high payoffs. The failure of government in recent years to ensure the high productivity of its investments has depressed total factor productivity to

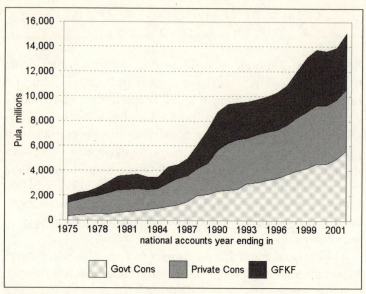

Figure 4.1
Absorption Components: constant 1993/94 prices
Source: Botswana Central Statistics Office, *National Accounts of Botswana.*

the point that, even if investment remains high, rapid growth rates will almost certainly drop to much more pedestrian levels. I now go on to consider each issue.

Macroeconomic Stability and Shock Absorbers

How successful was Botswana in achieving macroeconomic stability? The two major indicators most commonly looked at are (1) the stability of real domestic absorption and (2) inflation. Consider real domestic absorption. In a rapidly growing country such as Botswana, the relevant issue is not its absolute stability but, rather, the variation around the growth path. In Figure 4.1 I chart the three components of real domestic absorption: government consumption, private consumption, and gross domestic fixed capital formation.[2]

Looking at the individual components, it is clear that, for the most part, government consumption followed a stable growth path. There has been somewhat greater variation in

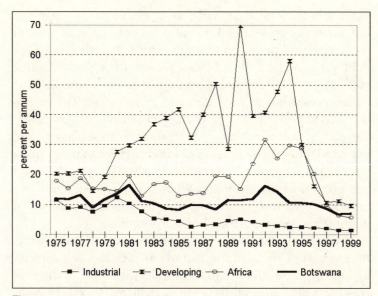

Figure 4.2
Inflation, Botswana and Comparisons
Source: International Monetary Fund, *International Financial Statistics.*

the path of private consumption, with the greatest year-to-year variation around long-run growth in gross domestic fixed capital formation. The acceleration of the latter two in the late 1980s is clearly associated with the rapid growth of credit (Figure 3.3), which, in turn, was encouraged by negative real interest rates. In brief, there have not been dramatic swings in real domestic absorption, but the paths of private consumption and gross fixed capital formation (including government's) have strayed from a sustainable path more than has the path of government consumption.

Turning to the second measure, inflation, the Botswana's historical record vis-à-vis that of groups of other countries is charted in Figure 4.2. If one compares Botswana with other developing countries as a group (or simply Africa), then Botswana's record is very good. If the industrial countries as a group are taken as the comparison, then, while Botswana kept inflation below the peaks hit by some individual industrial countries in the 1970s, its record in recent years is not as good. Finally, as already noted, Botswana has generally maintained an inflation rate close to that of its largest trading partner, South Africa (Figure 3.4).

In other words, Botswana's record of macroeconomic stability in the face of significant shocks – both to two major producing sectors (agriculture and minerals) and to the international terms of trade – is reasonably good. On various occasions a better performance could have been expected, but on no occasion did the macroeconomic imbalance reach the point where it seriously damaged the long-run growth of the economy. What was responsible for this felicitous outcome? The answer lies in the *combination* of institutions, policies, and shock absorbers.

In Chapter 3 we saw how government employed a wide-ranging array of institutions and policies to deal, directly and indirectly, with potential instability. Central to the process were the National Development Plans (NDPs). In addition, the standard tools of fiscal and monetary policy were deployed with varying degrees of success. Finally, the international trade and exchange rate arrangements played important roles.

Embedded in that experience is a feature that deserves to be highlighted: fiscal and monetary arrangements each created built-in shock absorbers. First, government, in effect, created a shock absorber between itself and the rest of the economy by absorbing revenue changes into its bank balance rather than into its spending. With government's revenues fluctuating dramatically, sometimes changing by 5% to 10% of GDP from one year to the next, government chose to keep expenditure growing at a slower rate than revenues. The result was that, starting in the mid-1980s, government began to accumulate significant credit balances with the Bank of Botswana (Figure 4.3). Government's credit balance at one point reached about 80% of GDP for the nation, which was almost two times government's annual expenditure and net lending.[3] Such substantial reserves in government hands created a shock absorber vis-à-vis the domestic economy, enabling government to keep

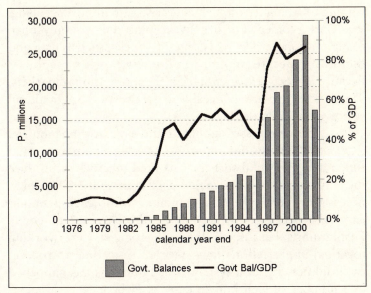

Figure 4.3
Government Balances
Source: International Monetary Fund, *International Financial Statistics.*

its expenditure and net lending reasonably close to a sustainable long-run growth path (Figure 1.6). An increase in revenue did not in itself initiate a new round of spending, while a drop in revenue did not force government to cut spending or take on debt. Had government spending followed government revenue closely after about 1985, dramatic year-to-year changes in spending would have been highly disruptive of the domestic economy.

Second, the aggregate expenditure discipline in the face of rapid export growth resulted in an accumulation of substantial foreign exchange reserves (Figure 1.7), which served as a shock absorber vis-à-vis the rest of the world. The foreign exchange reserves meant that private consumption and investment expenditures were able to evolve in the short-term independently of the potentially more erratic mineral export earnings and substantial year-to-year international terms of trade changes. The classic boom-bust cycle, starting with an import spending spree but ultimately leading to a balance of payments crisis and import licencing, was thus avoided. Further, by keeping the economy open to international trade, real domestic shocks, such as drought, did not generate significant domestic price responses because prices were anchored in the international markets. This was particularly noticeable in the case of the agricultural sector price deflator (Figure 1.4).

It is worth emphasizing that all three of these phenomena – effective institutions, appropriate policy responses, and functioning shock absorbers – worked together to produce the outcome. Much as each leg of a three-legged stool is necessary to keep the stool standing, so too each phenomenon was necessary to accomplish the observed outcome. Furthermore, because all three phenomena were working together, imperfections that emerged from time to time in each did not trigger a system-wide failure, as has happened in a number of well known cases elsewhere.

For example, the NDP process and the associated financial controls on government expenditure were important institutional arrangements that enabled government to stabilize expenditure growth while fluctuations on the revenue side were absorbed by changes in government balances. This, in turn, was only possible because government's accumulated cash balances had become an effective shock absorber.

At the same time, with the development of the Bank of Botswana's ability to absorb excess liquidity through the money market, reasonably stable and positive real interest rates followed, and the emerging capital market was not perturbed by swings in either government's fiscal balance or private-sector operating surpluses. For its part, the fixed exchange rate policy[4] meant that the bulk of the disturbances to the balance of international payments was absorbed by changes in the foreign exchange reserves while tradeables' prices were kept in line with world markets.

Note that the argument is *not* that all institutions were best practice – many were not; nor is it that all policies were always optimally calibrated for the circumstances – many were not; nor is it that all shocks were fully absorbed – not all shocks can be fully absorbed. Rather, it is important to recognize that institutions, policies, and shock absorbers all worked together to achieve the outcome.

Total Factor Productivity

It is clear from Chapter 1 that the rapid growth of real GDP has been associated with growth of inputs of labour and capital, and improvements in the health and education of the labour force (often referred to as human capital). However, it is not immediately evident what happened to the relationship between inputs and outputs – namely, productivity. The best overall measure is total factor productivity (TFP). This distinguishes growth of output that is attributable to increases in inputs from growth that is attributable to increases in productivity. Calculation of TFP is by no means an exact science; however, in essence it involves comparing the growth of output with the growth of weighted average inputs, with the difference between the two reflecting the growth of TFP.[5]

The results of the TFP calculations are summarized in Figure 4.4.[6] They reveal an average TFP growth of zero for Botswana over twenty-seven years from 1974/75 to 2001/02. This is less than the rate of about 1% comparable to some mature industrial countries and is certainly not in the same league as the rate of very fast-growing Asian countries.[7]

The full twenty-seven years masks some considerable variation over time. When the data are broken into five-year periods, they reveal a marked change. Initially, there was a big payoff from the heavy investment in infrastructure and human capital, with TFP growth of 3.7% for the first five-year period (1975–80). But the period from 1990 to 1995 reveals a significant *decline* in TFP of 2.7% per annum, recovering slightly to −1.0% per annum over 1995–2002.

What explains the dramatic fall? In part the effect is a statistical illusion. We saw in Figure 1.9 that government comprised the major component of additions to the capital stock, roughly doubling its share of the rapidly growing

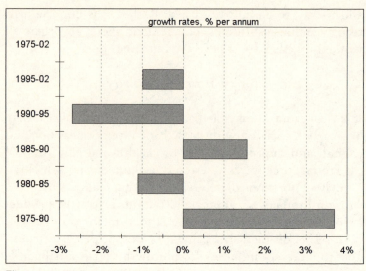

Figure 4.4
Total Factor Productivity Growth
Sources: See Appendix.

total real capital stock over twenty-five years. Since government-sector output is measured simply by counting the inputs, output grows at the same rate as do inputs, and therefore there is no increase in TFP from the now very large government sector.[8] Further, the diversification of the economy, to the extent that it was successful, involved an expansion of labour-intensive production of goods and services, with typically relatively low output per worker.

A third statistical explanation should also be noted. Our measures of inputs are of *potential* labour and capital inputs, not actual services provided. Hence, the substantial increase in the mining sector's capital stock in the early 1980s resulted in some significant excess capacity in that sector, particularly given the world recession that contracted demand just as much of the new capacity was coming into place. This helps explain the drop in TFP in the first half of the 1980s. Unemployment is not taken into account either. The phenomenon of youth unemployment, which began to appear in the 1990s, may have contributed to the TFP decline in the first half of the 1990s as well as

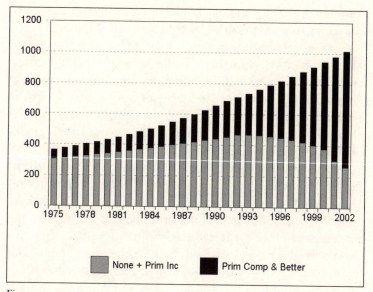

Figure 4.5
Education of Population 15–64 Years
Sources: See Appendix.

to the more rapid decline of TFP in the second half of the decade. Further, while AIDS may not have had a significant effect on the population and labour force numbers during the 1990s, it almost certainly had a negative impact on the effectiveness of labour, thus overstating the effective labour input and exacerbating the decline in TFP.

Despite these caveats about the data, the broad numbers provide a serious caution to Botswana's growth story. Over the twenty-seven years between 1975 and 2002, the capital stock grew at 9.1% per annum, the educated potential labour force grew at 9.6% (see Figure 4.5), yet output (net of mineral rents) grew at 7.8%.[9] TFP is now falling. In other words, Botswana's long-run growth story is fundamentally one of more and more physical and human capital investment that had an initial high payoff but that lead eventually to declining productivity.

What underlies this declining productivity? The basic explanation involves a set of adverse incentives. As noted in Chapter 3, monetary policy allowed borrowers access to commercial bank funds at negative real interest rates until late 1993. But even with the tightening of the money market, government programs continued to provide cheap capital through FAP. A further adverse incentive was the cheap capital made available through government loans (Figure 3.3) – directly to state-owned enterprises and indirectly to the public via state-owned financial institutions such as the National Development Bank and the Botswana Development Corporation.

The adverse incentives were not confined to the use of capital. For example, the agricultural sector continued to be favoured in the tax code even after the cheap capital via NDB dried up. Those earning employment income in the modern sector are permitted to continuously offset their tax liability by declaring losses on their farming operations, and the Botswana Meat Commission was granted a reduced tax rate in the mid-1990s.[10]

Another contributor to low productivity has been the failure of various institutions to adapt rapidly enough to the changing circumstances, thus creating growth bottlenecks. For example, the land allocation process, even after the corruption scandal in the early 1990s, continued to be cumbersome and slow. And, as noted in Chapter 3, during the 1990s the state-owned telephone company remained a bottleneck (as it had been in the 1980s), with new subscribers having a lengthy wait for service. Similarly, the post office had a queue for post office boxes.[11]

Botswana's Economic Record and the Virtuous Circle of Growth

Recall from Chapter 2 the idea of a "virtuous circle of growth," in which:

- a search mechanism identifies activities with high expected payoffs,
- investable resources are committed to those activities with high expected payoffs, and

• the process continues when realized high returns are reinvested in another round of high return activities.

Such a virtuous circle aptly describes the early years of Botswana's growth. The original search was focused primarily, but not exclusively, on mineral development. Many initially promising mineral discoveries proved uneconomic, but those that did well attracted significant investment from both foreign investors (in mineral extraction) and government (in infrastructure and human capital) – a substantial portion of which was at first financed by donors. The high initial returns were not simply consumed but were reinvested in further high return activities – both in minerals and elsewhere – by both the private and public sectors. This process continued for some time; however, on balance, the returns on investments in the 1990s proved to be declining. The virtuous circle of growth was breaking down.

2. INTERPRETING THE EVIDENCE: THE POLITICAL ECONOMY

The growth record is explained in the first instance by the economic policies that Botswana pursued. But the evolution of policies did not emerge from Botswana's blue sky: it was shaped by interests, institutions, and leadership – in brief by the political economy. Consider, therefore, the interaction between major policies on the one hand, and the nature of the institutions, interests, and leadership, on the other.

I start with the trigger – mineral policy. With no substantial mineral operation in place at the time of Independence, the Botswana government faced the formidable task of persuading a major foreign investor to sink funds into the search for and development of mineral deposits. Foreign investors in mineral projects bear a significant risk: the host government may engage in time inconsistent policies – agree to favourable terms today, but once the investment is sunk, renege and capture most of the returns. New governments are particularly prone to this behaviour. They urgently need to build support and therefore have very short time horizons. Khama's own royal heritage, which gave him a long-run perspective, the overwhelming electoral strength of the BDP, and the "diamonds-are-forever" horizon of DeBeers (the investor) all pointed in the same direction. An ongoing mutually profitable arrangement for sharing the mineral rents between the host government and the foreign investor was in the interests of both.[12]

The rapid growth of the mineral sector generated substantial rents for government. With the passage of time, the successful experience of the foreign investor helped to make the security of property rights more credible for all. Government's incentive to engage in time-inconsistent policies was reduced even more by this success, and its credibility was later reinforced when it bought into the foreign investor.

Government faced the choice of what to do with the proceeds of the mineral rents. The broad base of BDP support led government to use the proceeds initially to finance widely popular expenditure on broad national priorities – infrastructure and human capital – because these were the priorities of both the elite and the general population. The priorities of narrow specific interests were swamped by these general interests in the early post-Independence period. The fiscal linkage spread the growth throughout the economy, and the expenditures, in turn, served to reinforce the broad national support for the BDP.

The major concession of the BDP-led government to populist pressures was to tackle the favouritism associated with land allocation under the chiefs. The creation of tribal land boards gave legitimacy for the new democratic government without disrupting the traditional land tenure arrangements. Yet, as with any rationing system, the land board arrangement left in place the opportunity for corruption, which, on occasion, has surfaced.

The imperative of securing a major revenue source for government led to an early renegotiation of the terms of the Southern African Customs Union. In return, government accepted a major restraint on its discretion in trade policy. This obviated the creation of a specific interest that would have pushed the growth-retarding import-substitution policy that was followed in most other African countries. SACU kept the economy open to competition from imports while maintaining access to the regional market for some non-mineral exports.

Even more important politically, given the widespread ownership of cattle, was Botswana's participation in the European Union's Lome Convention. This yielded a higher than world price for a major portion of Botswana's beef exports – money that was largely passed on to cattle owners. Government bore the cost of an extensive system of controls over livestock movements in order to deal with the ever-present threat of foot and mouth disease entering from neighbouring countries.

Participation in the DeBeers-led marketing arrangement for diamonds – one of the few successful international commodity arrangements – achieved a further terms-of-trade gain for Botswana. Membership required the acceptance of periodic quota cuts, but the benefit of participation was so overwhelming that government never seriously contemplated an alternative to non-participation.

Money and financial sector policies, while not always ideal, generally provided stability to the macroeconomy. The cautious initial stance of remaining within the South African monetary area for the first decade of Independence was necessitated by the extreme shortages of trained personnel needed to run a central bank. Yet South Africa's initial refusal to share the seigniorage or the earnings on the foreign exchange reserves led to Botswana's monetary independence a decade after political Independence and to the evolution of an effective institution.[13]

The bulk of the population had a fundamental interest in monetary stability simply because financial savings were largely in the form of cash and bank deposits. The predatory instincts of privately owned banks were constrained by the central bank's licencing and supervision. The central bank's task of maintaining monetary stability was initially facilitated by the absence of a large specific interest in an inflationary policy. However, that configuration of interests was changing. The recycling of government mineral revenues through various public-sector financial institutions and schemes virtually eliminated the capital constraint for many parts of the economy, especially the state-owned enterprises and agriculture. An important new interest began to emerge – those who benefited from easy access to cheap capital and lax enforcement of payment arrears. Sometimes they succeeded in bending policy in their favour, as in the 1988 bailout of arrears allegedly attributable to the drought of the early 1980s. Further, state-owned financial institutions saw their roles as channelling funds to target clientele and, consequently, were ineffective in evaluating and monitoring projects. Later reform of the National Development Bank and the closing of the Co-operative Bank helped to staunch the haemorrhage of funds to unproductive investments. Had it not been for other binding constraints,[14] the demand for capital might well have absorbed a far larger portion of the mineral rents and foreign exchange reserves. The central bank's introduction of market-based monetary policy in the 1990s enabled it to maintain a modicum of monetary stability, but those with interests in cheap and easy access to capital became increasingly vocal in their demands.[15]

The decision to declare monetary independence also necessitated an exchange rate policy. The dominance of cattle ownership in the BDP's base constituency meant considerable support for the maintenance of a competitive real exchange rate, avoiding the peril of an overvalued currency commonly encountered following mineral discoveries or in polities dominated by import-substitution interests. Nevertheless, with the passage of time the emergence of an urban elite, with an interest in cheaper imports and other foreign currency-denominated payments such as foreign travel and education, began to compromise that policy thrust, and the pula was appreciated substantially in real terms against the rand (Figure 3.6).

Fiscal revenues were dominated by sources that did not appear to fall directly on the voters – minerals, customs, and foreign exchange reserves. Further, these revenue sources were not significantly distortionary. Hence, the revenue side was neither politically unpopular nor growth retarding.

Fiscal expenditure policy, on the whole, has been disciplined and growth-promoting. To a large extent this is attributable to the institution of the National Development Plans, reached through an elaborate consensus-seeking process and enforced by an effective institution of financial controls. This multi-year planning of government expenditures has, over the long term, kept government expenditure from growing as fast as government revenues. The resultant accumulation of substantial government savings and foreign exchange reserves has provided an important cushion to enable the country to ride out periodic diamond market downturns. The careful management of those reserves by the central bank – an effective institution created nearly a decade after Independence – generated a significant return to the nation.

Two other dimensions of fiscal discipline have been somewhat less successful. Government expenditure has grown to be one of the largest in Africa. It is arguable that this is not excessive relative to the revenue available to government, relative to many industrial countries, or relative to the openness of the economy.[16] Nevertheless, at the margin, many of government's expenditures are increasingly less effective in promoting long-run economic growth and human development. The other less successful dimension has been the difficulty government has faced in maintaining a stable growth path for its expenditure and net lending. There have been periods – such as 1988–92 and from the late 1990s – when government has contributed to inflationary pressures. In both cases, projects approved in the NDPs were allowed to bunch together in the early years of the plans, creating excess demand on the limited capacity of the economy, especially in the construction sector.

The consensus-seeking arrangement for the labour market was very effective in the early years. The extremes of an exorbitant real minimum wage and a bidding war for scarce talent were both avoided. The national interest in rapid growth dominated any one of the narrow sectional interests of employers, skilled workers, or unskilled workers. More recently, however, the expanding cadre of unskilled government employees has become more influential in its demands. The crowding out of private-sector employment and the emergence of youth unemployment both suggest that policies in these areas have not kept up with the rapidly evolving situation.

State-owned enterprises played an essential role in kick-starting the modern economy. Further, they did not become employers of first resort. Many of the SOEs were constrained from becoming a drain on society by the rules specified in their World Bank financing. Some that were not thus constrained, such as the housing corporation, became predators on the public purse as the interests of the urban elite came to have a growing influence on policy choice. At the turn of the century, with changing circumstances and technologies, there is no fundamental justification for the ongoing dominant role of many SOEs in their respective sectors. The challenge to phase out redundant SOEs – both financial and non-financial – or transform them into growth-promoting organizations, remains largely unmet. A white paper on privatization was published in 2000 (Botswana 2000), but in late 2003 only one major enterprise (Air Botswana) was nearing privatization.

Looking back over the post-Independence period, there has been a noticeable shift in government's thrust – from the provision of non-targeted goods and services towards the provision of specific rewards to particular interest groups. In part, this is attributable to the growing heterogeneity of economic interests in the country. Because interests are different, many policy initiatives no longer benefit everybody equally. In part, this shift is also attributable to the declining value of marginal public goods over the years.[17] Thus public goods have becomes less and less valuable to the general public at large. Meanwhile, the number of voters for whom a specific targeted benefit is worth more than the non-targeted public good has risen. Consequently, it is now more attractive for the dominant party to target specific benefits rather than to offer general benefits to the public at large. In a winner-take-all democratic political system, which Botswana's certainly is, this can lead to a discrete switch away from the provision of public-like goods towards the provision of specific benefits targeted at the dominant group's supporters.[18]

3. INTERPRETING THE EVIDENCE: DEMOCRACY

In Chapter 1 we saw that Botswana's democracy preceded growth, but per capita income growth has slowed and total factor productivity growth has plummeted. We saw in Chapter 2 that a democracy need not always produce optimal economic results. A democracy can produce political failure just as a free market can produce market failure. We also noted that the empirical cross-country growth literature finds very little evidence that democracy contributes to economic growth. Does the Botswana experience cast any light on the question of whether or not there is a relationship between democracy and growth?

The Botswana evidence suggests, first of all, that democracy alone is not sufficient to explain the country's rapid economic growth; rather, it is the *combination* of history, interests, and institutions, working within a democracy, that explains the Botswana case. Second, within this combination, the working of democracy helps to explain the rapid early economic growth and the subsequent slowing of growth. In the decade or two following Independence, the balance of economic policies focused on broadly based policies that were both widely popular and growth-promoting. As the influence of specific constituencies grew, the balance of policies favoured them. Such policies are seldom growth-promoting and, indeed, are often growth-retarding. Botswana's experience is no exception.

How serious has Botswana's political failure become? Botswana's democracy has certainly not lapsed into the authoritarian leadership extreme found all too frequently elsewhere in Africa – an extreme that repeatedly fails to yield sustained growth. Rather, Botswana's democratic political process has placed it in much the same position as that occupied by the democracies of major industrial countries. But Botswana's democracy has led to a new tension between the interests of those who have captured the power of the state (to further their own ends) and those who have not.[19] That outcome has yielded slower growth and only modest reductions in poverty.

4. SUMMING UP

I set out to determine why Botswana prospered. Was it luck or is there an explanation based on some identifiable influence? In searching for an answer, I reviewed the economic and political record, and examined Botswana's policy evolution in the context of some basic ideas about the sources of growth and the roles of interests and institutions. It is now time to sum up this evidence and to provide a short, coherent answer to the original question.

Botswana's exceptional growth record is explained in the first instance by the economic policies that it pursued. In most of the major policy areas growth-promoting policies dominated. The economic record is not explained by a single silver (or diamond) bullet; rather, it is explained by a whole range of policies that worked together and were supported by effective institutions.

Minerals policy, itself the product of Botswana's fledgling technocracy working within the consultative tradition, generated the rents that initiated growth. Government's long-term development planning was crucial in channelling funds into investments that promoted both growth and human development, and in maintaining a modicum of fiscal discipline. Given this fiscal discipline, it was possible for the central bank, a post-Independence institution, to accumulate and manage substantial foreign exchange reserves, and to pursue a disciplined monetary policy. This combination of fiscal and monetary discipline, in turn, made it possible for trade policy to keep the economy open and for exchange rate policy to encourage the emergence of non-traditional exports and import-competing production. At the same time, the policy combination created shock absorbers that helped to stabilize the economy in the face of the instability of real output in major sectors and international terms of trade. In other words, it was not simply the choice of good policies that promoted growth: for these policies to work, Botswana also had to build and maintain effective institutions.

Not all of the policies promoted growth and human development. The shortcomings of labour market policies, the slow pace of reform of SOEs, the real exchange rate appreciation, and the large size and uneven growth of government are all serious problems. Indeed, if prompt action is not taken to redress these failures, then Botswana risks a period of sustained stagnation. Nevertheless, the record of accomplishment in pursuing a set of policies that has proven to be growth-promoting for more than three decades cannot be contested.

These policies were shaped by the leadership, but within the context of interests and institutions that had their origins in traditional Tswana society and were modified during the Protectorate. The initial leadership of Seretse Khama was profoundly influenced by his own royal background, which had instilled in him a sense that privilege entails responsibility, the ethnic diversity of his own tribal territory, and the strong traditional culture of compromise. Yet he and the BDP were also responding to interests in an emerging democratic society. Initially, the interests were mostly homogeneous and were based on cattle, thereby creating an overwhelming encompassing interest. This, in turn, made it easier to achieve consensus on policies that were growth-promoting and helped to transform an ethnically diverse society, albeit with largely homogeneous interests, into a modern democracy. And, in that modern democracy, the habit of consensus seeking is thoroughly ingrained.

The rapidly growing economy contributed to the ongoing ability of the BDP to maintain political dominance, to reinforce the growth-promoting bias in economic policy, and to reinforce government's interest in maintaining a democratic system. Yet growth created its own tensions for, as the economy grew, specific interests emerged. These increasingly heterogeneous interests competed to divert policy in their own favour, making policy choice more complex. As economic policy becomes bent in favour of particular interests rather than in favour of the aggregate interest, future growth is at risk. But the competition inherent in the functioning democracy has made it less likely that those specific interests will succeed in capturing the state's power solely for their own ends. The challenge remains: to share the fruits of growth among *all* Batswana.

Finally, what role did luck play in the outcome? Was it "something in the water"?

There are certainly specific instances of good luck, such as the discovery of diamonds shortly *after* Independence. But, on the other side, there are examples of bad luck, such as Botswana's landlocked location, surrounded at Independence by hostile white-ruled regimes. It is not luck – good or bad – that explains Botswana's story: what explains Botswana's story is that the *right combination* of influences emerged at the right time to shape the country's development. In the fledgling democracy, interests and effective institutions, moulded by history and leadership, shaped growth-promoting economic policies. Had any part of this set been missing, Botswana's story would have been notably different. There *is* something in the water. Pula!

Total Factor Productivity Calculations

The rate of growth of total factor productivity is the rate of growth of total output less the weighted average rate of growth of factor inputs.

The real output series for the national accounts years 1974/75 to 2001/2002 was reported in Figure 1.2. Included in the value of output is the mineral rents – the difference between the opportunity cost of the inputs and the value of the output. Since rents clearly are not attributable to the inputs of capital and labour, I have corrected the output series by deducting the value of the mineral rents, proxied by the government's mineral revenues (Figure 3.8), deflated by the GDP deflator to constant prices.

The real capital stock series for the same period was reported in Figure 1.8.

There is no comprehensive series that covers the labour input for the entire economy for the same period. However, the population census reports the population aged fifteen to sixty-four years and the labour force for each of the census years. The CSO, in turn, has calculated the population by age group for the inter-censual years. Thus, assuming the labour force share of the population fifteen to sixty-four years changes at a constant rate between censuses, it is possible to calculate the labour force each year. The population censuses of 1964, 1981, 1991, and 2001 were used for the total population. (The census of 1971 was omitted because of significant under-enumeration.) The total population of the intervening years was interpolated, and then the shares of the population fifteen to sixty-four and the shares of that population in the labour force were applied to the interpolated population. The share of the population fifteen to sixty-four was assumed to continue at the 2001 share for 2002. Note that this is a measure of the *potential* labour force as it does not adjust for unemployment. The labour force is divided into skilled and unskilled on the basis of the shares of educational attainment of the population, as reported in the censuses (Figure 1.10). The resulting skilled and unskilled potential labour force is shown in Figure 4.5.

The factor shares were calculated from the cso, *Social Accounting Matrix*, for 1985/86 and 1992/93 and averaged. In calculating the factor shares the mineral rents noted above were first deducted from the net operating surplus.

Notes

CHAPTER ONE

1 See Easterly and Pritchett (1993) for an elaboration of the evidence that rapid economic growth is typically short-lived.
2 See Sachs and Warner (1995).
3 For further elaboration, see Leith (1997a).
4 For 1967/68 the mining sector was defined so as to include mineral exploration and development. The cost of materials purchased exceeded operating revenues, resulting in a negative value added and, therefore, a negative share of GDP.
5 For example, Gelb (1988) documents the difficulties that several producing countries had with the oil price shocks of the 1970s.
6 The net lending was mostly in the form of long-term loans to state-owned enterprises. See Chapter 3, Section 3 for further discussion.
7 See Hill and Knight (1999) for a more extended examination of Botswana's adjustment to diamond booms and slumps.
8 While expenditure plus net lending has followed trend growth since the mid-1990s, during the late 1990s government expenditure itself resumed rapid growth. The consequences in terms of the share of government in the economy will be taken up below.

9 I return to the issue of government as shock-absorber in Chapter 4.

10 The numbers reported in Table 1.2 reflect a very modest effect of AIDS on the population. The life expectancy figures for 2001 may be overstated, largely because the *reported* numbers of cases of AIDS and deaths attributable to AIDS at the time the estimate was prepared were relatively small. See below for further discussion.

11 Interestingly, the NDP *for 1973–78* contains no tables detailing the numbers of such services.

12 NDP 8, published in 1997, cites the incidence as 23% of the sexually active population ages fifteen to forty-nine (p. 402). Research summarized in BIDPA (2001) places the estimate for the year 2000 at 38.5% of those aged fifteen to forty-nine.

13 The United Nations Development Program (UNDP) estimates that the adjustment for AIDS has dropped life expectancy at birth to forty-six years from sixty-seven years (see UNDP 2000). Some other international agencies put the life expectancy figure much lower. However, as noted in Table 1.2, the 2001 census reports that life expectancy has only fallen to fifty-nine years.

14 Budget Speech 2001, paragraphs 50–3.

15 BIDPA (2001) base case indicates that the growth rate of GDP per capita would actually increase by a small amount over what it would have done without AIDS but that less favourable assumptions would reduce the growth rate of GDP per capita.

16 Data for 1991 and 1993/94 are reported in NDP 8, p. 55. The census data include unpaid workers, usually family members, in the economically active population.

17 The others are: sustained development, rapid economic growth, and economic independence.

18 The third HIES was conducted in 2002/03, but results had not been released by the end of 2003. The 2002/03 HIES will reflect the effect of a universal old age pension introduced in 1996. For those receiving the destitute's allowance, the old age pension is additional (from 1997).

19 The relatively high unemployment rate of 1993/94, noted above, has subsequently declined substantially. Since most of the unemployment is concentrated in the urban areas, it is likely that the Gini coefficient has also declined.

20 Central Statistics Office (CSO), 1991.

21 CSO HIES 1993/94, 6. This comparison excludes a third group – those resident in traditional villages now classed as urban because less than 25% of the labour force is engaged in agriculture.

22 There is no third group (urban villages) and the data include non-citizens, which account for a little less than 3% of the sample.

23 The term "tribe" is employed in Botswana to mean a polity under the umbrella of a kgosi (loosely translated as chief, or king). To avoid endowing the term with a precise meaning I use "tribe," "polity," and "state" interchangeably. See Ramsay, Morton, and Morton (1996) for elaboration.

24 See Campbell and Tlou (1984).

25 Tlou (1998) sketches the secession of various groups to form their own tribes and emphasizes how subjects could leave if a chief did not keep them, and especially potential leaders of dissident groups, satisfied with his rule. This was not unique to the Tswana tribes, however. Herbst (2000) argues that lack of pressure on land and ease of exit profoundly influenced state building throughout Africa.

26 See Tlou (1985).

27 Ibid., 2.

28 There is a notable parallel with similar patterns among those indigenous groups within North America (e.g., the Cree), where land did not support dense population concentrations and where variable weather patterns resulted in a high variance of income from year to year.

29 See, for example, Tlou's (1985, 47–50) description of the assimilation by the BaTawana in Ngamiland.

30 For considerable detail on the traditional land tenure system, see Hitchcock in Picard (1985).

31 One of the most serious crimes was stock theft, for which severe penalties were, and still are, meted out.

32 A brief gold rush had occurred near modern-day Francistown in 1867–69 but did not prove nearly as rich as the later rush in the Transvaal.

33 See Fawcus and Tilbury (2000).

34 Quoted from the British High Commissioner by Fawcus and Tilbury (2000, 21).

35 Prior to 1934, and the establishment of "Dominion" status for the Union of South Africa, the governor general of South Africa was the British High Commissioner. See Parsons in (Picard) 1985.

36 There were also some non-tribal areas, arising from specific concessions in the past, where only the Protectorate Government had jurisdiction.

37 In one celebrated case a Kalanga leader, John Nswazwi, was imprisoned and later exiled by Tshekedi Khama, long-time regent of the Bamangwato. Nswazwi died in exile in 1960. See Ramsay 1987a.

38 For example, in 1931 Sebele II, chief of the Bakwena, was deposed by the British and banished to Ghanzi (located in the far western part of the Protectorate) until he died in 1939. See Ramsay 1987b.

39 Included in the Protectorate's local revenue sources was revenue from the Southern African Customs Union (as compensation for the fact that the Protectorate was not collecting customs duties itself). The customs union agreement was renegotiated after Independence, at which time compensation was substantially increased.

40 Fawcus's assessment on taking up his post as government secretary in 1954 (see Fawcus and Tilbury 2000, 48).

41 Curiously, there seems to have been no attempt to determine the wishes of the residents of the Protectorate.

42 Fawcus and Tilbury (2000, 60).

43 When the pre-Independence political parties were founded, the initial "B" stood for Bechuanaland, which became Botswana at Independence.

44 While that choice might seem so obvious as to not require any decision, at the time Bechuanaland was surrounded by regimes without such a system.

45 One, Bathoen II of the Bangwaketse, chose the route of politics in 1969, defeating Vice-President Masire, who was returned to Parliament by the use of the constitutional provision that permitted the president to appoint up to four "specially elected" members of Parliament.

46 It is noteworthy that in the next census, held in 1964 in preparation for the 1965 elections, the question of tribal affiliation was not asked.

47 The Census Table II(f) lists the numbers for each subtribe in each tribal territory. At that time the Tswana prefixes Ba- (to refer to Tswana) and Ma- (to refer to non-Tswana [literally, "falling outside the human class"]) were employed in the listing, facilitating the breakdown between Tswana and non-Tswana. Due to its derogatory overtones, the prefix Ma- is no longer employed for official purposes.

48 The San were also about the same proportion in Ngamiland, the home of the Batawaṇa, where, similar to the Bamangwato, the ruling principal Tswana tribe had only 20% of the total population. It should be noted that the San themselves are not a homogeneous group. There are many different San languages, some of which are mutually unintelligible.

49 This includes just over 1% of the total, consisting of "European," "Coloured," and "Asiatics." In addition, since the ethnic composition of the Africans living outside the tribal territories (just under 5% of the total) was not broken down, I have arbitrarily split this group between "Other Tswana" and "Non-Tswana" to calculate the percentage distribution of the total population.

50 Mauro (1995, Appendix 3), reports the ELF index for Botswana as fifty-one, whereas our calculations using the 1946 census data yields an ELF of fifty-five.

51 The Mochudi result also reflects the influence of the chief, Linchwe II, whose opposition to the BDP was widely known.

52 Koma later became the titular leader of the BNF.

53 In 2001 Koma retired as leader of the BNF, but the squabbling continued between Koma's faction and the new leadership.

54 This is also cited in the literature as the Gastil index, after the compiler.

55 Amnesty International did, however, condemn Botswana for the 2001 use of the death penalty in the case of a South African woman who had been convicted of murder in Botswana.

56 In the 2002 report the index was 6.4 and the ranking was just behind that of Portugal, while in the 2001 report the index was 6.0, with a ranking between Ireland and France. One of the factors contributing to the slippage in the index may be the failure of government to proceed with a proposed requirement that all members of Parliament disclose their assets.

57 Nevertheless, after having had difficulties enforcing libel actions against some parts of the press, in 2002 government indicated its intention to regulate the mass media via registration, accreditation, and monitoring of the press.

58 More recently (in 2001), the Bamalete, one of the eight principal Tswana tribes, chose a woman as chief.

59 Holm's first constraint might better be thought of as an incentive for every chief to ensure that his rule had broad public support. The second constraint meant that a new chief was not free to set his own constitutional rules.

60 An alternative interpretation, which I take up in Chapter 3, is that this outcome was the result of the constitutional rule of winner take all.

61 Yet he never makes explicit which interests were affected by which policies or that the provision of public goods was in response to the incentives facing the ruling party leadership.

62 I return to this issue in Chapter 4. Samatar fails to recognize that it is in the collective interest of the leadership and the dominant class to control the extent of the rent-seeking and corruption so that the total pie can be maximized. Such an outcome may be attributable to weak leadership and/or the high discount rate, and it could be labelled a "political failure" as defined in Chapter 3.

CHAPTER TWO

1 I am indebted to James Robinson for discussion of these issues.

2 This issue is well known to those who contemplate why the United Nations General Assembly comes to quite a different balance of outcomes than does the International Monetary Fund and the World Bank. It is the difference between the outcomes of one-member/one-vote and one-dollar/one-vote.

3 Note should also be made of Solow's doubts concerning cross-country regressions involving large numbers of countries. First, "If they mean anything at all, those many right-hand-side variables in growth regressions are determinants of TFP [total factor productivity] ... [Second,] the proper measure of output underlying the left-hand-side variable is potential output. ... [Third,] many countries, much of the time, are nowhere near steady-state growth. This suggests that comparative studies should focus less on the growth rate and more on comparing and understanding whole time paths," including their "different institutional histories" (Solow 2001, 286–8).

4 The institutionalist thrust is not new, of course, for it builds on a school associated with the name of John R. Commons (1934).

5 Predation is simply plundering. In addition to outright thievery, this economic concept refers to any waste of real resources such as might occur in rent-seeking (Krueger 1974), smuggling (Sheikh 1974), and/or what Bhagwati (1982) characterizes as directly unproductive profit-seeking activities. The cost is more than simply the cost of a distortion (such as a tariff) that arises from a suboptimal allocation of resources; rather, the cost is the equivalent of taking part of society's output and burning it.

6 Wintrobe's (2001) review of Olson's book suggests that the stationary bandit concept "makes more sense if two

assumptions are made: (1) the dictator has only economic objectives (i.e., she is interested only in money); (2) she is securely in office, and faces no effective competition for her position" (393).

7 Two titles illustrate the thrust of this argument: Joel Migdal's (1988) *Strong Societies and Weak States*; and Peter Evans's (1992) "The State as Problem and Solution: Predation, Embedded Autonomy, and Structural Change."

8 I use the term "regime" to refer to the ruling group that controls government policies and actions.

9 Even dictatorships face the need to bolster support. See Wintrobe (1998).

10 Another problem may arise: unless the number of regime leaders entitled to participate in the patronage pool is strictly limited, participation in the pool will expand, thereby further diluting the benefit to individual members.

11 This discussion draws on Leith and Lofchie (1993), who apply the common property resource concept to explain why the Ghanaian regime of the 1970s pursued economically destructive policies far beyond any reasonable political optimum.

12 Bates (1999) has a helpful exposition of this point.

13 In terms of the discussion of the virtuous circle of growth, noted above, the return on the high-payoff activity is not reinvested in the economy, thereby breaking the circle.

14 The classic public good is law and order, including the protection of property rights.

15 Weingast (1995) emphasizes that not all agreements can be enforced ex-post, and different political systems have varying degrees of success in organizing institutions to deal with the problem. More generally, as Drazen (2000) makes clear, the sequential nature of policy making together with some ex post heterogeneity of interests are necessary for time inconsistency to arise.

16 For example, Collier (2001) finds that ethnic diversity is not damaging when government is a democracy.

CHAPTER THREE

1 Recall that many of the chiefs, headmen, and counsellors supported Seretse Khama and the BDP because the latter was seen as the more likely to represent their interests than was the BPP. In subsequent elections the BNF, which became the principal opposition party, attempted to build a bridge across a coalition ranging from chiefs to workers. However, for the most part, it failed to do so.

2 BDP Election Manifesto, 1965, 5.

3 P. 37. The original also includes the Setswana term for each principle.

4 They are also known as San, or Bushmen. Note that "Basarwa" is a Setswana term but uses the general plural prefix in place of the derogatory one that had been used before Independence. Among the Basarwa themselves, there is no consensus on the appropriate name for their ethnic group (which consists of several different language groups).

5 The Bechuanaland Protectorate Development Plan 1963/1968, mentions the potential development of copper, coal, and soda ash, all of which were located in the Bamangwato tribal territory.

6 See National Development Plan 1973–78 for further details.

7 In addition, over the years government purchased additional shares in Debswana (the Botswana operation of DeBeers). Further, in 1987 the Botswana government used part of the proceeds from the sale of an accumulated stockpile of diamonds to purchase 5% of the shares of DeBeers itself. In 2001, when DeBeers moved from being a publicly traded company to a privately held company, the shares held by the Government of Botswana roughly doubled the government's share of the equity.

8 In the 1990s mining of gold deposits in the Francistown area was reactivated.

9 It did, however, generate considerable employment for mine workers, most of whom would otherwise have been

working in South African mines. For more details on mineral policy and background on the diamond and copper-nickel developments, see Harvey and Lewis (1990) and Gaolathe (1997).

10 Further, while the individual was free to raise the matter in the *kgotla*, the fact that the chief was presiding and that the wealthier members had considerable influence in the *kgotla* discussions reduced the odds of a successful appeal.

11 See *Report of the Presidential Commission of Enquiry into Land Problems in Mogoditshane and Other Peri-Urban Villages* (Botswana 1991).

12 Namibia was included in the territory of the customs union during its administration by South Africa. When Namibia was granted independence in 1990 it became a full-fledged member of the union.

13 The new Southern African Customs Union Agreement, initialled in late 2001, will, when implemented, change the compensation arrangement. Rather than an open-ended commitment by South Africa, the new agreement will only distribute revenue from the common external tariff and excise taxes.

14 There is a special provision for granting temporary "infant industry protection" to specific new industries against imports from all sources (including elsewhere within the SACU), but it has been used only in a few cases and generally with disappointing results.

15 For more details on Botswana's trade policies, see Leith (1997b).

16 For more details, see Hudson (1978) and Hermans (1996).

17 Paragraph 24(c) of government's white paper, *A Monetary System for Botswana*, Government Paper No. 1 of 1975, March (Botswana 1975).

18 Bank of Botswana, *Annual Report 1993*, 17.

19 For more details on the evolution of monetary control in Botswana, see Majaha-Järtby (1998).

20 It should be kept in mind that the data are annual average CPI inflation rates. Since each country has a different basket

of consumer items in its index, even if monetary policies were identical, one would not expect the rates to coincide exactly.

21 Most prominent among these was the rental rate on housing provided by the state-owned enterprise. See discussion below.

22 Another important influence on Botswana's inflation rate was the exchange rate policy, considered in the next section (see Leith 1991).

23 Responsibility for and ownership of their operation was switched from their South African headquarters to their British parents.

24 For further discussion of Botswana's exchange rate policy, see Leith 1991 and 1996.

25 Mogotsi (2002) detected some evidence of relative (but not absolute) decline in some manufacturing industries, which she attributes to real currency appreciation.

26 Of course, if a dollar-based foreign investor were producing a good or service that depended on the health of the domestic economy, then the two effects would tend to offset each other.

27 For more detail see Mohohlo (1997).

28 For more detail see Modise (1999).

29 Since the reference point for most residents is South Africa, the tax on consumers in Botswana implicit in SACU membership is not directly evident to the consumer.

30 There are concessional company tax rates of 15% that apply to some qualifying manufacturers and to the new financial services centre.

31 Since 1979, the period has been six years.

32 The data are drawn from World Bank, *World Development Indicators 2000*, Table 4.12. The very high number for Lesotho arises because the denominator is GDP, which in Lesotho's case excludes mineworkers' remittances, which, in turn, are spent, generating government revenue under the SACU.

33 The relatively easy access of the elite to medical treatment in South Africa may have reduced pressure on government

to provide such facilities in Botswana. Further, in the early 1990s a private hospital was established in Gaborone.

34 The comparative data are from *World Development Indicators 2000*. The statistics do not provide the basis for anything more than very rough comparisons, as not all countries are as meticulous as Botswana is in reporting all military expenditures as such.

35 See *National Development Plan 1973–78* (Botswana, various dates). The reference to sustained production was later changed to "sustained development."

36 See Government Paper No. 2, *National Policy on Incomes, Employment, Prices and Profits* (Botswana 1972).

37 Ibid., 5.

38 Ibid.

39 That linkage is no longer explicitly included in setting the minimum wage rate.

40 Initially, government demanded that all graduates from the University of Botswana work for government on the grounds that it had paid for their education. This was later eased and then abandoned.

41 It should be noted that changes in earnings may be due to other effects, such as changes in composition of either government or manufacturing. However, no data on wage *rates* are available.

42 Figures for military employment are not included in the total and are not published.

43 Following the incomes policy review of 1990, this began to change.

44 See Bank of Botswana, *Annual Report 1995*, 66. These data were collected by the 1993/94 Household and Income Expenditure Survey. Since the primary purpose of the survey was not to measure unemployment, the data should be assessed with some caution. Estimates of the unemployment rate for 2000, as noted earlier, stood at just above 15%.

45 The comparability of data may be a problem in this area also. In some countries the state is a major shareholder, but the enterprise does not function as a classic "state-owned enterprise," while in others, with a minority shareholding,

the state may have effectively taken over the direction of the enterprises. Note that the Botswana government's shares in the DeBeers Botswana Company are *not* included in the SOE category.

46 This does not imply, however, that the parastatals were not overstaffed.

47 Since some of the loans were to state-owned financial institutions, to eliminate double counting, the figure cited omits them. If one takes the entire outstanding loans, the amount would be 13.8% of GDP at the end of fiscal 1997.

48 Source: author's own calculations from Bank of Botswana, *Annual Report 2000*.

49 For example, the NDP 1968–73 contains a section entitled "Private Enterprise," which notes "the expansion of the industrial base – presently very small – is a prime objective of Government policy" (para. 2.16).

50 For example, the NDP 1979–85, published in 1980, ten years after the establishment of the BDC, had a modest list of seven potential major projects with a total capital investment of P23.8 million, of which the BDC would invest P5.7 million. Total employment anticipated in those major projects would be 1,060.

51 *Industrial Development Policy*, Government Paper No. 2, October 1984.

52 Ibid., para. 43.

53 *Financial Assistance Policy*, Government Paper No. 1, March 1982.

54 Para. 55.

55 *Daily News*, 4 June 2001.

56 Source: Bank of Botswana, *Annual Report*, various years.

57 The capital of NDB was negative by the end of March 1992 (Bank of Botswana, *Annual Report, 1993*), and government's equity at the end of March 1993 was also negative (1994 *Budget Speech*, para. 56).

58 Calculated as the average annual payment to government plus retained earnings for the fiscal years ending March 1991 through 2000, as a percentage of the average of government's equity participation in the BDC over the same

period. (Sources: BDC, *Annual Report 2000*, Table entitled "Value Created"; and Bank of Botswana, *Annual Report 2000*, Statistical Tables 5.2 and 7.7.)

59 For more detail, see Good and Hughes (2001).

60 The 2001 Budget Speech noted: "Botswana Development Corporation has nearly completed its operational and financial restructuring in line with its Strategic Plan of 1998. As a result of the restructuring exercise, the Corporation turned around from a loss making position to achieve a net profit of P19.5 million in 1999/2000" (para. 37). The details of the losses and restructuring were not specified but can be gleaned from the BDC balance sheet. From the end of March 1998 to the end of March 2000, BDC's reserves dropped from plus P231 million to minus P30 million. During the next quarter government evidently converted P100 million of its loan outstanding to BDC into equity (see Bank of Botswana, *Annual Report 2000*, Statistical Table 5.1.).

CHAPTER FOUR

1 On macroeconomic stability see, for example, Fischer (1993). On the role of investment in growth, see World Bank (1999).

2 I exclude changes in stocks from my measure of absorption. In Botswana such changes are dominated by changes in inventories of minerals, which are not influenced by domestic policy considerations.

3 From 1997 onwards, the credit balance includes the portion of the revaluation gains on the foreign exchange reserves notionally attributable to government. In turn, the credit balance was reduced in 2002 when government used a significant portion of it to cover its unfunded liability for the Public Officers Pension Fund, which it had been meeting on a pay-as-you-go basis. At the end of 2002 the credit balance had been reduced to a little more than one year's expenditure and net lending.

4 As noted in Chapter 3, the exchange rate was fixed to a basket and was not infrequently adjusted in light of

changing circumstances. Nevertheless, surges of net foreign exchange earnings and spending had little influence on the exchange rate itself, unlike under a freely exchange floating rate.

5 TFP is thus essentially a residual that contains the errors of measurement of both inputs and outputs.

6 The TFP calculations reported here are *not* the same as reported in Leith (1997a). The present calculations employ revised GDP data as well as new capital stock data, and they cover five more years. See Appendix for details.

7 Young (1995) reports TFP growth for Hong Kong 1961–91 at 2.3% per annum, and for Taiwan 1966–90 at 2.1% per annum. Young's numbers are considerably more detailed than this, however.

8 To the extent that value added per worker is higher in the government sector than in declining sectors such as agriculture, the process of transferring inputs to government is likely to increase economy-wide TFP.

9 The picture is much the same if we simply look at real GDP and real capital stock for the economy as a whole, *excluding* government and mining.

10 In the 1995 budget speech the tax rate on the Botswana Meat Commission turnover was dropped from 35% to 15%, while in the same budget the company profits tax was reduced to 25%.

11 The queue for post office boxes was a serious problem for new businesses as there is no postal delivery in Botswana. All mail must be collected either from a post office box or poste restante.

12 In technical terms, given the low discount rate for Botswana and DeBeers, respectively, the present value of the future benefit stream from the sharing arrangement vastly outweighed any alternative for each, such as confiscation (by Botswana) or abandoning the country (by DeBeers).

13 Hudson (1978) notes that, after Botswana announced its intention to withdraw from the Rand Monetary Area, South Africa came to an agreement with the other members, Lesotho and Swaziland, and did agree to share seigniorage.

14 Recall that among the important constraints were the covenants on World Bank loans to the public utilities, the shortage of skilled personnel, and the continued membership in SACU.

15 Two incidents illustrate this: (1) In the mid-1990s, as real interest rates moved from mildly negative to mildly positive, the president of the Botswana Confederation of Commerce Industry and Manpower publicly led efforts to persuade the Bank of Botswana to ease up on its policy of maintaining real interest rates in line with major international financial markets, while simultaneously serving as a member of the central bank's board. (2) In 2001 the introduction of a bill to Parliament involving a minor change in the legislation governing the National Development Bank was met with a barrage of criticism from MPs from all parties, who complained that the NDB's interest rates and security requirements were now too high.

16 Rodrik (1998) shows that more open economies have larger governments.

17 For example, the first 100 kilometres of paved highway was very valuable to the entire economy because it was put on the busiest route. But continuing to pave more and more roads ultimately means that the marginal paving projects are worth very little to society as a whole.

18 In the simple model of Lizzeri and Persico (2001) a winner-take-all political system switches from the provision of public goods to benefits targeted at supporters when the value of the targeted benefits exceeds the value of the non-targeted (public) goods for the majority.

19 Good (1999 and 2002) argues that the elite have rewarded themselves, not the marginalized ones.

References

Acemoglu, D., and J.A. Robinson. 1999. "On the Political Economy of Institutions and Development." *American Economic Review* 91, 4: 938–63.

Acemoglu, D., S. Johnson, and J.A. Robinson. 2000. "The Colonial Origins of Comparative Development: An Empirical Investigation." *American Economic Review* 91, 5: 1369–1401.

Adam, C.S., and S.A. O'Connell. 1999. "Aid, Taxation and Development in Sub-Saharan Africa." *Economics and Politics* 11, 3: 225–53.

Aghion, P., and P. Howitt. 1998. *Endogenous Growth Theory*. Cambridge, MA: MIT Press.

Alesina, A. 1998. "The Political Economy of High and Low Growth." In *Annual World Bank Conference on Development Economics 1997*, ed. B. Pleskovic and J.E. Stiglitz, 217–37. Washington, DC: World Bank.

Aron, J. 2000. "Growth and Institutions: A Review of the Evidence." *World Bank Research Observer* 15, 1: 99–135.

Bank of Botswana. Various years. *Annual Report*. Gaborone: Bank of Botswana.

– 1985. *Tenth Anniversary, 1975–1985*. Gaborone: Bank of Botswana.

Barro, R.J. 1997. *Determinants of Economic Growth: A Cross-Country Empirical Study*. Cambridge, MA: MIT Press.

Bates, R.H. 1999. "Institutions and Economic Performance." Paper delivered at Conference on Second Generation Reforms, Washington, DC, IMF.

Baumhogger, G. 1999. "Botswana." In *Elections in Africa: A Data Handbook*, ed. D. Nohlen, M. Krennerich, and B. Thibaut, 103–21. Oxford: Oxford University Press.

Bechuanaland Democratic Party. 1965. *Election Manifesto*. Reprinted in W.J.A. MacCartney, *Select Documents on the Government and Politics of Botswana, Lesotho and Swaziland*. Roma, Lesotho: UBLS Printing Unit, 1971.

Bechuanaland Protectorate. 1963(?). *Development Plans 1963/1968*. Mafeking(?): Bechuanaland Protectorate.

Besley, T., and S. Coate. 1997. "An Economic Model of Representative Democracy." *Quarterly Journal of Economics* 112, 1: 85–114.

Bhagwati, J.N. 1982. "Directly Unproductive, Profit-Seeking (DUP) Activities." *Journal of Political Economy* 90, 5: 988–1002.

Botswana Central Statistics Office (CSO). *Botswana Agricultural Statistics*, various years. Gaborone: CSO.

– *Census 1971, 1981, 1991*, and *2001*. Gaborone: CSO.

– Botswana Central Statistics Office. *Household Income and Expenditure Survey: 1985/86*, and 1993/94. Gaborone: CSO.

– 1976. *Rural Income Distribution Survey, 1974/75*. Gaborone: CSO.

– *National Accounts of Botswana 1971–72*. Gaborone: CSO.

– *National Accounts of Botswana, Revision of 2001*. Gaborone: CSO.

– *Stats Update*, occasional. Gaborone: CSO.

Botswana. Various dates. *National Development Plan*: No. 8, 1997–98 – 2002–03. No. 7, 1991–1997. No. 6, 1985–91. No. 5, 1979–85. No. 4, 1973–78. No. 3, 1970–75. No. 2, 1968–73. *Transitional*. Gaborone.

– 1972. *National Policy on Incomes, Employment, Prices and Profits*. Government Paper No. 2. Gaborone.

– 1975. *A Monetary System for Botswana*. Government Paper No. 1 of 1975. Gaborone.

– 1991. *Report of the Presidential Commission of Enquiry into Land Problems in Mogoditshane and Other Peri-Urban Villages*. Gaborone.

– 2000. *Privatisation Policy for Botswana*. Government Paper No. 1. Gaborone.

– Annual. *Financial Statements, Tables and Estimates of the Consolidated and Development Fund Revenues*. Gaborone.

Botswana Independent Electoral Commission. 1999. *Report to His Honour the Vice-President and Minister of Presidential Affairs and Public Administration on the General Elections*. Gaborone.

Botswana Institute for Development Policy Analysis (BIDPA). 1997. *Study of Poverty and Poverty Alleviation in Botswana (Phase One)*. Gaborone: BIDPA (for Rural Development Coordination Division, Ministry of Finance and Development Planning, Botswana Government.)

Briscoe, A., and H.C.L. Hermans. 2001. *Combating Corruption in Botswana*. Gaborone: Friedrich Ebert Foundation.

Campbell, A.C., and T. Tlou. 1984. *History of Botswana*. Gaborone: Macmillan Botswana.

Caves, R.E. 1965. "'Vent for Surplus' Models of Trade and Growth." Chapter 6 in *Trade, Growth, and the Balance of Payments*: Essays in honor of Gotfried Haberler, ed. R.E. Baldwin et al. Chicago: Rand McNally.

Chenery, H.B., and A.M. Strout. 1966. "Foreign Assistance and Economic Development." *American Economic Review* 56, 4, pt. 1: 679–733.

Collier, P. 1996. "The Role of the African State in Building Agencies of Restraint." In *New Directions in Development Economics*, ed. M. Lundahl and B.J. Ndulu, chap. 12. London: Routledge.

– 2001. "Ethnic Diversity: An Economic Analysis." *Economic Policy* 30 (April): 128–66.

Commons, J.R. 1934. *Institutional Economics: Its Place in Political Economy*. New York: Macmillan.

Cowan, D. 1997. "The Selibi-Phikwe Regional Development Project: A Case Study of the Costs and Benefits of Foreign Direct Investment." In *Aspects of the Economy of Botswana: Selected Papers*, ed. J.S. Salkin, D. Mpabanga, D. Cowan, J. Selwe, and M. Wright, 549–69. Oxford: James Currey.

Crick, B. 1989. "Keynote Speech: On Democracy." In *Democracy in Botswana: Proceedings of a Symposium held in Gaborone, 1–5 August 1988*, ed. J.D. Holm and P.P. Molutsi, chap 5. Gaborone: Macmillan Botswana.

Crowder, M., J. Parson, and N. Parsons. 1990. "Legitimacy and Faction: Tswana Constitutionalism and Political Change." In *Succession to High Office in Botswana*, ed. J. Parson, chap. 1. Athens Ohio: Ohio University.

Datta, K., and A. Murray. 1989. "The Rights of Minorities and Subject Peoples in Botswana: A Historical Evaluation." In *Democracy in Botswana: Proceedings of a Symposium held in Gaborone, 1–5 August 1988*, ed. J.D. Holm and P.P. Molutsi, chap. 10. Gaborone: Macmillan Botswana.

Davis, K., and M.J. Trebilcock. 1999. "What Role Do Legal Institutions Play in Development." Paper delivered at Conference on Second Generation Reforms, Washington, DC, IMF.

Diamond, L., J.J. Linz, and S.M. Lipset. 1988. *Democracy in Developing Countries*. Vol. 2: *Africa*. Boulder, CO: Lynne Rienner.

Drazen, A., 2000. *Political Economy in Macroeconomics*. Princeton, NJ: Princeton University Press.

duToit, P. 1995. *State Building and Democracy in Southern Africa: Botswana, Zimbabwe, and South Africa*. Washington, DC: United States Institute of Peace.

Easterly, W., and L. Prichett. 1993. "The Determinants of Economic Success: Luck and Policy." *Finance and Development* 30(December): 38–41.

Easterly, W., and R. Levine. 1997. "Africa's Growth Tragedy: Policies and Ethnic Divisions." *Quarterly Journal of Economics* 112, 4: 1203–50.

Engerman, S.L., and K.L. Sokoloff. 1997. "Factor Endowments, Institutions, and Different Paths of Growth among New World Economies." In *How Latin America Fell Behind*, ed. S.H. Haber, chap. 10. Stanford, CA: Stanford University Press.

Evans, P. 1992. "The State as Problem and Solution: Predation, Embedded Autonomy, and Structural Change." In *The Politics of Economic Adjustment: International Constraints, Distributive Conflicts, and the State*, ed. S. Haggard and R.R. Kaufman, chap. 3. Princeton, NJ: Princeton University Press.

Fawcus, P., and A. Tilbury. 2000. *Botswana: The Road to Independence*. Gaborone: Botswana Society and Pula Press.

Fidzani, N.H. 1998. "Land Reform and Primitive Accumulation: A Closer Look at the Botswana Tribal Grazing Land Policy." In *Botswana: Politics and Society*, ed., W.A. Edge and M.H. Lekorwe, chap. 15. Pretoria: van Schaik.

Fischer, S. 1993. "The Role of Macroeconomic Factors in Growth." *Journal of Monetary Economics* 32, 3 (December): 485–512.

Gaolathe, B. 1997. "Development of Botswana's Mineral Sector." In *Aspects of the Economy of Botswana: Selected Papers*, ed. J.S. Salkin, D. Mpabanga, D. Cowan, J. Selwe, and M. Wright, 401–31. Oxford: James Currey.

Gelb, A. and associates. 1988. *Oil Windfalls: Blessing or Curse?* New York: Oxford University Press. (for the World Bank.)

Good, Kenneth. 1997. "Authoritarian Liberalism in Botswana." In *Realizing Democracy in Botswana, Namibia and South Africa*, ed. K. Good, chap 1. Pretoria: Africa Institute of South Africa.

– 1999. "The State and Extreme Poverty in Botswana: the San and Destitutes." *Journal of Modern African Studies*. 37, 2: 185–205.

– 2002. *The Liberal Model and Africa: Elites against Democracy*. Houndsmills, UK: Palgrave.

Harberger, Arnold C. 1998. "A Vision of the Growth Process." *American Economic Review* 88, 1: 1–32.

Harvey, Charles, and Stephen R. Lewis, Jr. 1990. *Policy Choice and Development Performance in Botswana*. New York: St Martin's Press.

Herbst, J. 2000. *States and Power in Africa: Comparative Lessons in Authority and Control*. Princeton, NJ: Princeton University Press.

Hermans, H.C.L. 1996. "The History of the Bank of Botswana." *Bank of Botswana Research Bulletin* 14, 2: 1–48.

Hill, C., and J. Knight. 1999. "The Diamond Boom: Expectations and Economic Management in Botswana." In *Trade Shocks in Developing Countries*. Vol. 1: *Africa* , ed. P. Collier and J.W. Gunning, chap. 9. Oxford: Oxford University Press.

Hitchcock, R.K. 1985. "Water, Land and Livestock: The Evolution of Tenure and Administration Patterns in the Grazing Areas of Botswana." In *The Evolution of Modern Botswana*, ed. L.A. Picard, chap. 5. Lincoln: University of Nebraska Press.

Holm, J.D. 1988. "Botswana: A Paternalistic Democracy." In *Democracy in Developing Countries*. Vol. 2: *Africa*, ed. L. Diamond, J.J. Linz, and S.M. Lipset, chap. 5. Boulder, CO: Lynne Rienner.

Holm, J.D., and P.P. Molutsi, eds. 1989. *Democracy in Botswana: Proceedings of a Symposium held in Gaborone, 1–5 August 1988*. Gaborone: Macmillan Botswana.

Hudson, Derek J. 1978. "The Establishment of Botswana's Central Bank and the Introduction of the New Currency." *Botswana Notes and Records* 10: 119–35.

Krueger, A.O. 1974. "The Political Economy of the Rent-Seeking Society." *American Economic Review* 64: 291–303.

Leith, J.C. 1992. "The Static Welfare Effects of a Small Developing Country's Membership in a Customs Union: Botswana in the Southern African Customs Union." *World Development* 20, 7: 1021–8.

– 1996. "Botswana's Exchange Rate Policy." *Bank of Botswana Research Bulletin* 14, 2: 125–9.

– 1997a. "Growth and Structural Transformation in Botswana." In *Aspects of the Economy of Botswana: Selected Papers,* ed. J.S. Salkin, D. Mpabanga, D. Cowan, J. Selwe, and M. Wright, 21–35. Oxford: James Currey.

– 1997b. "Botswana's International Trade Policies." In *Aspects of the Economy of Botswana: Selected Papers*, ed. J.S. Salkin, D. Mpabanga, D. Cowan, J. Selwe, and M. Wright, 529–48. Oxford: James Currey.

– 1999. "The Design of Policy Frameworks and the Role of the Policy Advisor." In *Rationality in Public Policy* ed. R.M. Bird, R.M. Trebilcock, and T.A. Wilson, 141–57. Toronto: Canadian Tax Foundation.

Leith, J.C., and M.F. Lofchie. 1993. "The Political Economy of Structural Adjustment in Ghana." In *Political and Economic Interactions in Economic Policy Reform*, ed. R. Bates and A.O. Krueger, chap. 6. Cambridge, MA: Blackwell.

Lizzeri, A., and N. Perisco. 2001. "The Provision of Public Goods under Alternative Electoral Incentives." *American Economic Review* 91, 1: 225–39.

Majaha-Jartby, J. 1998. "Adoption of Indirect Instruments of Monetary Policy in Less Developed Financial Markets – The Case of Botswana." *Research Bulletin* (Bank of Botswana) 16, 2: 1–10.

Mauro, Paulo. 1995. "Corruption and Growth." *Quarterly Journal of Economics* 110, 3: 681–712.

McKinnon, R.I. 1973. *Money and Capital in Economic Development*. Washington, DC: Brookings.

Migdal, J.S. 1988. *Strong Societies and Weak States: State-Society Relations and State Capabilities in the Third World*. Princeton, NJ: Princeton University Press.

Modise, M. 1999. "Managing Mineral Revenues in Botswana." In *Development Policies in Natural Resource Economies*, ed. J. Mayer, B. Chambers, and A. Farooq, 78–97. Cheltenham: Edward Elgar.

Mogotsi, I. 2002. "Botswana's Diamond Boom: Was There a Dutch Disease?" *South African Journal of Economics* 70, 1: 128–55.

Mohohlo, L.K. 1997. "Central Banks as Protectors of National Wealth: Botswana's Case." In *Aspects of the Economy of Botswana: Selected Papers*, ed. J.S. Salkin, D. Mpabanga, D. Cowan, J. Selwe, and M. Wright, 241–71. Oxford: James Currey.

Ngcongco, L.D. 1989. "Tswana Political Tradition: How Democratic?" In *Democracy in Botswana*, ed. John Holm and Patrick Molutsi, chap 8. Gaborone: Macmillan Botswana. (For Botswana Society.)

North, D.C. 1990. *Institutions, Institutional Change and Economic Performance*. New York: Cambridge University Press.

Olson, M. 1993. "Dictatorship, Democracy, and Development." *American Political Science Review* 87, 3: 567–76.

– 1996. "Big Bills Left on the Sidewalk: Why Some Nations Are Rich and Others Poor." *Journal of Economic Perspectives* 10, 2: 3–24.

– 2000. *Power and Prosperity: Outgrowing Communist and Capitalist Dictatorships.* New York: Basic Books.

Parsons, Q.N. 1985. "The Evolution of Modern Botswana: Historical Revisions." In *The Evolution of Modern Botswana: Politics and Rural Development in Southern Africa,* ed. L.A. Picard, chap. 2. London: Rex Collings.

– 1998. *King Khama, Emperor Joe and the Great White Queen: Victorian Britain Through African Eyes.* Chicago: University of Chicago Press.

Peters, P. 1995. *Dividing the Commons: Politics, Policy and Culture in Botswana.* Charlottesville, VA: University Press of Virginia.

Picard, L.A., ed. 1985. *The Evolution of Modern Botswana: Politics and Rural Development in Southern Africa.* London: Rex Collings.

Picard, L.A. 1987. *The Politics of Development in Botswana.* Boulder, CO: Lynne Rienner.

Przeworski, A. 1991. *Democracy and the Market.* New York: Cambridge University Press.

Ramsay, J. 1987a. "The Neo-Traditionalist: Sebele II of the Bakwena." In *The Birth of Botswana: A History of the Bechuanaland Protectorate from 1910 to 1966,* ed. F. Morton and J. Ramsay, chap 2. Gaborone: Longman Botswana.

– 1987b. "Resistance from Subordinate Groups: Babirwa, BaKgatla Mmanaana, and BaKalanga Nswazwi." In *The Birth of Botswana: A History of the Bechuanaland Protectorate from 1910 to 1966,* ed. F. Morton, and J. Ramsay, chap. 4. Gaborone: Longman Botswana.

Ramsay, J., B. Morton, and F. Morton. 1996. *Historical Dictionary of Botswana.* London: Scarecrow Press.

Rodrik, D. 1998. "Why Do More Open Economies Have Bigger Governments?" *Journal of Political Economy* 106, 5: 997–1032.

– 1999. "Institutions for High Quality Growth: What They Are and How to Acquire Them." Paper delivered at Conference on Second Generation Reforms, Washington, DC, IMF.

Sachs, J.D., and A.M. Warner. 1995. "Natural Resource Abundance and Economic Growth." Development Discussion Paper

No. 517a. Cambridge, MA: Harvard Institute for International Development.

Samatar, A.I. 1999 *An African Miracle: State and Class Leadership and Colonial Legacy in Botswana Development*. Portsmouth, NH: Heinemann.

Schapera, I. 1953. *The Tswana*. London: Kegan Paul. (Reprinted 1991.)

Scoville, J., and T. Nyamadzabo. 1988. "Report of the Impact of Minimum Wages in Botswana: Prepared for NEMIC, Government of Botswana." Gaborone.

Schultz, T.W. 1961. "Investment in Human Capital." *American Economic Review* 51, 1: 1–17.

Sheikh, M.A. 1974. "Smuggling, Production, and Welfare." *Journal of International Economics* 4, 4: 355–64.

Solow, R.M. 1956. "A Contribution to the Theory of Economic Growth." *Quarterly Journal of Economics* 70, 1: 65–94.

– 1957. "Technical Change and the Aggregate Production Function." *Review of Economics and Statistics* 39: 312–20.

– 2001. "Applying Growth Theory across Countries." *World Bank Economic Review* 15, 2: 283–8.

Stiglitz, J.E. 1988. "Economic Organization." In *Handbook of Development Economics*, vol. 1, ed., H. Chenery and T.N. Srinivasan, chap. 5. Amsterdam: North Holland.

Tlou, T. 1985. *A History of Ngamiland, 1750 to 1906: The Formation of an African State*. Gaborone: Macmillan Botswana.

– 1998. "The Nature of Batswana States: Towards a theory of Batswana traditional Government – the Batawana case." In *Botswana: politics and society*, ed. W.A. Edge and M.H. Lekorwe, chap 2. Pretoria: van Schaik.

Transparency International. 2003. *Corruption Perceptions Index*. Berlin: Transparency International.

United Nations Development Programme (UNDP). 1998. *Botswana Human Development Report 1997*. Gaborone: UNDP.

– 2000. *Botswana Human Development Report 2000*. Gaborone: UNDP.

Weingast, B.R. 1995. "The Economic Role of Political Institutions: Federalism, Markets and Economic Development." *Journal of Law, Economics, and Organization* 11, 1: 1–31.

Wintrobe, R. 1998. *The Political Economy of Dictatorship*. New York: Cambridge University Press.

– 2001. "Review of Mancur Olson (2000)." *Public Choice* 106: 390–5.

Wittman, D. 1989. "Why Democracies Produce Efficient Results." *Journal of Political Economy* 97, 6: 1395–424.

World Bank. 1989. *Botswana: Financial Policies for Diversified Growth*. Washington, DC: World Bank.

World Bank. Various years. *World Development Indicators*. Washington, DC: World Bank.

World Bank. 1999. *World Development Report 1999/2000*. Washington, DC: World Bank.

Young, A. 1995. "The Tyranny of Numbers: Confronting the Statistical Realities of East Asian Growth Experience." *Quarterly Journal of Economics* 110 (3): 641–80.

Index

83–8, 117; expenditure and net lending, 9f, 125n8; expenditure, comparisons, 85f; expenditure, composition, 86f failure. *See* political failure; investment, 103, 104, 113; knowledgeable ministers, 56; labour market, and, 88–93; loans to state-owned-enterprises, 72, 73f, 75, 112, 126n6; planning, 117, 120; purchasing, 98, 99; revenues, 81–2, 82f, 83f; shock absorber, as, 106–8; technical assistance to, 57; working of, 56–9

government consumption, 104, 104f

growth: Botswana comparisons, 4t; constraints, 42; cross-country regressions, 47; democracy, and, 41–53, 119–20; innovations, and, 42; neoclassical, 42; real GDP per capita, 4; theory, 41–3; vent for surplus, 42; virtuous circle of, 43

Harberger, 42
Harvey, 143n9
health, 15–16; primary health care, 15; services, 16f
. *See also* HIV/AIDS
Herbst, 127n25

Hermans, 35, 134n16
Hill, 125n7
Hitchcock, 67, 127n30
HIV/AIDS, 15–16, 126nn10, 12, 13
Holm, 35, 37, 130n59
House of Chiefs, 27–8
Household Income and Expenditure Surveys (HIES), 17, 126n18, 127n21
Howitt, 42
Hudson, 139n13, 143n16
Hughes, 138n59
human development, 14–6. *See also* education; health

income distribution, 17–9; Gini coefficient, 17, 18t; rural-urban differences, 19. *See also* Household Income and Expenditure Surveys
industrialization policy, 97–101; abuse of incentive programmes, 99; incentive programmes, 98–9. *See also* FAP, SPRDP, CEDA; Industrial Development Policy, 99, 137nn51, 52; rationale, 97
inflation, 10, 74–5, 75f, 85, 105–6, 105f, 135n22; Botswana and South Africa, 75f, 85. *See also* monetary policy
institutions, 47–53, 106; agencies of restraint, as, 52; combination of: and history, and inter-

ests, 119, and interests and leadership, 113, and policies, 106, 108–9; conflict management, for, 52; effective execution, 50; factor endowments, and, 51; history, and, 51; interests, and, 51–2; leadership, as, 49–50; public goods, and, 51; settler colonies, and, 20–1, 51; technocracies as, 51
interest rates. *See* monetary policy
interests, 43–7; capital, 55; cattle, 30, 55, 116, 121; cheap capital, 116; encompassing, 48, 54, 121; exchange rate, 55, 116; heterogeneity of, 45; homogeneity of, 55, 122; labour, 55; land, 55; monetary stability, 115; overvalued currency, 116; targeted goods and services, 45, 118
international trade, 68–70, 106, 108, 114, 121

Johnson, 51
judiciary, 36, 59

Kalanga, 24, 36, 128n37
kgosi, 127n23
kgotla, 20, 27, 28, 36, 134n10
Khama: Chief, III, 25; Ian, 33; Seretse, 22, 25–8, 31, 33, 37, 39, 40, 44, 56–7, 60–1, 114, 121;

Transparency Inter-
national, 34–5,
130n56
Trebilcock, 48
Tswana: age regiments,
20; assimilation of
non-Tswana, 21;
Bamangwato, 25,
29; chiefs, 20; domi-
nance of, 24, 28–9,
59; history, 19–22
Tswapong, 36

unemployment, 16–7,
92–3, 127n19,
136n44

virtuous circle of
growth, 43, 112–3,
132n13

wages: average
monthly earnings,
91f; formal sector,
88–90

Warner, 125n2
Weingast, 47, 132n15
Williams, Ruth, 26
winner-take-all, 45
Wintrobe, 131n6,
132n9
Wittman, 44
World Bank, 80, 95,
118, 135n32,
136n34

Young, 139n7